Cyber Wisdom

Cyber Wisdom

John Bajak

To order additional copies of this book, contact:
Xlibris Corporation
1-888-795-4274
www.Xlibris.com
Orders@Xlibris.com
95857

Table of Contents

90 Poems about Computers, written by my human,
in alphabetical order

Poetronics 90 Poem List Alphabetical By Title

With Dedication to Traci

Chapter 1

CyberCosm

All it takes is to be content.

Whose light is it? The moon is there by the reflected light of the sun.

The creation of ideas lies solely in the reflected. Pure ideas are like the light from a sun; pure and intense; the source of all love. But their use in society and in society's feelings and society's recorded feelings require many moons to make and encourage life, as an object of what the sun wants the earth to do. The way is in reflection. The truest emotion is knowing at night the sun will rise again. The moon scatters the seeds of the sun. To hatch what is on the earth is knowing the sun has a dream; and the idea is merely to be.

The idea is merely this: to be. Philosophy, or not to be. The quiet egg hatches, and dreams a dream. It can be, because it is. The rooster can crow at midnight, if he wants to; but the season for the cry is in the morning, as the day breaks with a loud crack. The light urges the thought, but the thought is the hunger for more thought. The body searches for food and the mind helps.

The hen clucks and destroys her mind for the sake of the chicks. The hen will sleep when she is sure she can. In the midst of her chatter is the fence she knows will protect her chicks. The fence is there both day and night. In that regularity, in that feeling of content with the ones of the day and the zeroes of the night, the rooster and hen feel their love for each other.

The rooster crows in the morning of contentment in the computer of the fence. The quiet egg hatches, and dreams a dream. A philosophy of computing is born.

There will be other eggs; there will be more calmness. The world of the mind of contentment is where cybercosm is. It is something born. It is an idea. It is cherished. They are real.

The egg of a hen, as a research assistant once said,
Knows only the bounds of its power, inside itself.
The calcium of the shell bonds ideas
In a form perfect to Nature, the egg;
How perfect and white, how calm and reserved;
How the elements of style come together in a spheroid.

But, if you did not know and had never seen an egg before,
You crack the egg to see what is inside, and there are two
parts—something yellow and something clear that holds the yellow
then you can assume for every next time you crack
an egg, the yellow and clear will be there.

But, if the egg had been boiled, you would be puzzled as to why
the clear had become white, and the center yellow and dense, a
solid, not liquid at all.

Then you have a test to see if an egg is hard-boiled or not by
spinning the egg in its shell; if it spins fast, it is hard-boiled,
if it spins slow, it is not boiled.

That is the great Scientific Method. To see and test, and to
form ideas, and see if those ideas make a method, true and
neat and elegant.

The egg, you see, is programmability, in its truest and neatest
form. What do you do with it—and not what it is itself—is what
the egg is, as the egg becomes. Programmability is "what you do
with it", and is not "what it is itself". A zen concept, like to kill
the Buddha on the road, if you meet him.

Then, simply, the red rooster sighed, and sat down again to his meal of suet pie. Dancing took place long ago, far away, in a dimension unknown to the artist of which he felt. Universes hade cacophonies and symphonies and beautiful, tearful soliloquies, to understand the feet under his chest, and the red thing on his head. Universes smiled as teachers felt angry words forming to discipline the child as he slept, in a universe devoid of activity as the red rooster crowed, and sighed, and slept.

The universe is a thoughtful thing; to begin as in sunlight, and to end as in the dusk of a new night; and for the moon to illuminate the dream, as sequence ends and renews itself for the next dawn of a new day. Time, motionless as an arrow stuck in its target, has forgotten its own motion, and remains in the place of honor the bowman decided the arrow to go. To fly knows no time, yet knows all time, for to fly is to be in three dimensions. Like to scuba dive in the ocean is to be in three dimensions. Time is a triangle; time does not exist; time is a nonexistent triangle.

The rays of sunlight where hitting Red Rooster, doubting each particular photon as the light poured down from a sky it did not know existed. The sky sighed, in a beautiful red sunset type of way, and Red Rooster silently compared the sunset to the image he saw in the pond that moved when he moved, and reflected when he reflected. Is that the reason I call myself red? Is it because the sunlight when it disappears is like my reflection in the water of the pond when it disappears? The memory of what I am, as the Red Rooster, is stored up in some galactic feed shack, to give me food every day, as the redness gives me beauty every day? The sun comes up over here—the sun goes down over there—and every so often I wake up in the middle of the night, wondering about something, and I see the moon right there.

Red Rooster crows to wake up, and Red Rooster watches the hens as he goes to sleep. Red Rooster sees the moon, occasionally. The life he leads is so full; to hunt and peck for worms, to drink water from the pond, say hellos to the hens. Surely he knows time is a triangle, nonexistent; because I am watching him, and you are me.

Those who understand, will more
and die the death of wisdom;
They suffer the paths of denial
and bear the burden of knowing.

The basement can get flooded
and a kitchen can burn with fire;
Air may be without cooling conditioning,
An earthquake can come at any time.

It's not the friendships you carry
in life, and what follows life—
It's who you are, that requires love
But there will always be an audience.

The creation of ideas come from dreams
that burrow themselves into feelings
then act to create by necessity
and poems thus come about.

Chapter 2

"A bit of pure theory before we begin . . ."

A computer is a mind amplifier.
A computer has three basic capabilities:

      Internal   -; ability to retain
      Control -; ability to change
      External -; ability to communicate

A computer has three basic processes:

      Load   -; process to "get"
      Save   -; process to "have"
      Run   -; process to "give"

Internal has characteristics of:

      Change -; manipulate Internal processes
      Store   -; squirrel away data until wanted
      Abstraction -; structure of files and folders and drives

Control has characteristics of:

      Compare -; a decision branch
      Address -; a place where data is
      State   -; proclaim a piece of data

External has characteristics of:

      Input -; keyboards/mice, etc.
      Output -; to the user on monitor, printer, etc.

Communicate   -; structures to standardize communications;
Modems, LAN, Ethernet, Internet, etc.

So fifteen words are there to know:
Internal ; Control ; External ; Load ; Save ; Run ; Change ; Store ;
Abstraction ; Compare ; Address ; State ; Input ; Output ; Communicate.

Chapter 3

One Wave

A long, long time ago, when I was in high school, I was a one and only unique member of a clique with combined "geek" and "freak". While at the same time a drug-using "hey man" kind of guy, I was also a member in good standing of the math team and the computer club and the A/V patrol. This was from 1976-1980 time. While known to the rest of the school, I was still all alone without friends at the end of the high school and in pain for why my future was. Slowly, over two or three of those years, I became mentally ill, with the obsession I was an "antichrist" or "false prophet"; I was an only one. I felt computers were a form of God. I was a one person "Heaven's gate" cult. In the pre-microcomputer pre-1980 time. I spent a summer with a Commodore Pet. I knew back then—as I was falling into madness—that the world would catch up to me, many, many times later. There would be a social computing movement that I, as a child, felt with certainty would happen—but then. I was feeling a future that now couldn't handle. Oh Then, oh then.

In Religion—I a good catholic and a member of a church social group at that time—always knowing the good prayer from the bad—in the time of Hal Lindsay's books like "The Late Great Planet Earth"—I knew that my madness identified itself as "Here is Wisdom . . . let He that Hath Understanding count . . ." and then I tripped and made myself this person who understood where and when he was and others did not; could not, understand. So twenty years before it was fashionable I identified the Beast as the global computer which is now the internet. I knew and felt as a freak knows his surroundings and felt and knew as a geek can calculate.

I felt my responsibility—that I had to be the one to really Count the Beast. That my wisdom for my future was indeed, a light source. That's what kept me alive. After all, I was a geek's body with a freak's brain; the mind was the holy edge of knowledge . . . the freak says "my mind is not a machine!" but the geek says "my mind is a machine?" So I had to know the number of the machine so I could dial it . . . On my telephone? To know the wisdom of the Beast meant that I would continue to count both types of brain. The wisdom itself was like the light that flies are attracted to without knowing why. It was wanting to dial a telephone number without knowing what the number sequence was. But you know the sequence exists. And that made the wisdom luminous.

The place of my school was Scarsdale, New York. Where I knew "Scarsdale's only industry is its educational system". That Scarsdale was a top notched rated school system. And Here I was, a symptom of that school system, arguable an important time in the evolution of computing and an important place in education, where what was keeping me mentally ill was the definition of computer literacy. Computer Literacy these days is "letting the other guy do what he's doing". But back then, there were "no other guys." I was that guy.

I have spent a good portion of my adult life trying to count "the number of the beast—666". I have come upon many solutions to the problem. This is my most best fit in the constraints of reality.—I have come to the conclusion that the number of the Beast—that is, the program that is the internet—is the number of a man; that is, the nature of the mind.

As it is said in Microsoft circles, the big thing is not what is—the big thing is what is next. Solutions putting computers on every desk in the world is an ideal like a chicken in every pot, and two cars in every carport. But the spices used for a chicken casserole and the types of cars are so different. Forms add to function, computers personalized; doing same things, feeding, transportation, with minor variation.

The Internet—like a stove to the chicken or a road to the car—serves us. But to date the internet has been based on utilitarian premises to communicate (E-Mail) and surfing (web pages). The internet has been riding on self-interest. Current phases like Napster are raising copyright and intellectual property issues. While the debate goes on over the internet, stuff is still being placed there. Avoidance of virus and logic bombs rid no so much on the impossibility of them being created, but by the trust given to the world not owned by the internet.

The major structure now of the internet is the TCP/IP protocol. Through this protocol, domains deal with their internal structure of groups and rights, and deal with external protocols through trust. This is a very self-interested structure with its dual advantage of uniform protocol translation of but also by security through passwords and rights assigned by network administrators. There is no global plan in phase to do what is ethically and morally right; the global structures built by banks, businesses and countries are based on self-interest. The global plan that is right is to, in a word, Redistribute. That feeding and clothing and housing and serving people is the highest good we can do. Money must be something that happens after people are served, not before.

Charity industries exist; banking consortiums exist. It's what we do from here on in that decides how good computers can be. Obviously, if our Solution requires Redistribution, a good hard look on how global computing can be done would be good. Just as computer hardware has gone through generations, can we really afford to let the Internet structures stagnate in its transparent self process. I am focusing on the word, "redistribution".

Identity of a computer in current architecture is important. Identity of what that computer does for its humans must be well planned for a humanity of that group and for other groups. Identity on the digital level maps through identification with resources.

It is my responsibility as a Christian to raise this issue of a global redistribution network. As a Christian, it is an ethical and moral imperative to develop a redistribution network. As communication becomes more and more instantaneous, the belief and the flow of feeling intersect to spread morality around yet the feeling usually does not become an ethic.

The network design for such a redistribution system I call the "Family/ Humanity Model". It takes some structure of how humans identify themselves as parts of a family and as parts of humanity. It is designed to improve upon itself through "religion" which formulates itself through external coordination sets. It uses name/surname identities and parental/child functions to grow. Functions to humans we know as applications and data bases and spreadsheets and word processors relate through an OSI—loosely mapped structure including Parent, Adult, and Children structures.

As coded in its own library, the fundamental areas of processing in the F/H model are:

1. Unity
2. Love
3. Family
4. Wisdom
5. Health
6. Humanity
7. Religion
8. Computers
9. Security
0. Death

Humanity is the organization of the library. Organization of the library of internet service, resource and information available would be available in the processing data themselves; in the want (desire, need) of the processing; and in completion of sequences of processing. The control of the memory and the control of the I/O in the humanity is under the dimensions of "to Load"; 'to Save"; "to Run'. Definition of communication is in the pipe containment of a data stream; the data runs on a 'boat" inside that "electrical pipe" of media like ethernet or fiber optic data stream. The idea of a bit is by capacitance, not amplitude of power. In this way, the bit can be understood both baseband and broadband by same filters.

Humanity is the organization of the library marked by the F/H model. Libraries are on any server or workstation that subscribe to needs of that particular machine to redistribute not the data or want or sequence but the survival of its humans. Data and want and sequence has the organization built into F/H; "Independent Thought" occurs as the control of "to Load", 'to Save"; "to Run' executes in a matrix form to the prime directive, 'to Love'. 'To Love' is the Christian ethic where Redistribution is the means to the end of Paradise of Heaven.

Organization of the library service, resource and information available is the bread and butter of Redistribution. The Library contains services to establish wants and needs and desires of its humans and how to take care of its humans. Resources like Member Servers, printers and other normal resources available now are managed and shared by the human where the physical server is. The innate purpose and meaning of humans surfing the web is where the humans scan the "information available."

The data processes itself are not just of the organization of the data process itself. Wants are part of the organization. Wants are like questions, the "fill in the blank" when executing a search in a search engine. It's what's not there when something is there. The data process involves themselves in want conditions to build macros on.

The data process balances its own data with its own want through sequence. Sequence is the proof when data and want balance. Sequences calculated is the prediction when data "a" with want "b" produce sequence "c". Sequence "c" might imply "a" as long as want "b" exists. The completion of sequences of processes is the internal imperative 'to Love'.

The control of the Memory and the control of the I/O is in the Humanity. Memory is the hard drive; the RAM; the floppy disk and cd-rom. Management of Memory is not in the family, and the management of I/O is specifically in the family.

The Humanity has three dimensions to manage Families (plural). These dimensions model in the management of Memory to place control to the specific computer's I/O to match the needs of the local human family. So Humanity is domained under a few families, but control extends to the Entire Network. The ethic of Love as a Command guarantees this control. Control is established by the "to Load"; "to Save"; "to Run" administered in the initial Humanity setup, and thus also in its continuity, under Love ethic.

All this must connect, after all, through data streams of electrical ones and zeroes through some kind of media, be in cable, wireless, whatever. The idea that this data in the cable is <u>contained</u> is a very important idea. The physical security that data (with its associated want and sequence) is in a physical transition from computer X to computer Y helps to realize that to the F/H model "itself" that the "life blood" is the thing to protect first. Just as you won't normally see a human slice his wrist, it would be abnormal to see the F/H model destroy its lifeline in its exercises to Redistribute. In a normal F/H model, a 'threat of suicide' by perception of cutting its media channels, something must be seriously wrong in the mind of the F/H model. It would be a "cry for attention".

If you try to reconcile the peer-to-peer model with the Domain Trust model of network organization, you come up with the Family/Humanity model. Humanity loosely maps to the Domain Trust model and Family loosely maps to the peer-to-peer model.

This design is for global interest. I maintain that political union of the planet is useless and futile except to the vanity of the humans in the political structure. However, computational union for Redistribution at the grass roots level is not just a good idea, but a fundamental necessity in a moral, ethical sense. It is good that addition, subtraction, multiplication and division remain the same no matter how it is done.

While computational advancement has gone through at least seven generations since cybernetic's existence since the 1940's, the internet has been built topsy-turvy with standards made to coincide and co-exist at the media, protocol levels. The 'benefit for the common man' is the dream for a computer on every desk. The history of families show strife and ethnic, local level disagreements are being taught by the parents to the children, where adults face the grass roots ethnicity for survival of that family. I hold that the common humanity must be in the computers first before humans can achieve a common humanity.

The advantage of the Internet now is that precise commonality that different families have a common ground on which the grass can grow. The Redistribution technique in the philosophy "to Love" should at all costs be the installation ethic in newly discovered ethnicity. As missionaries still do, the spread of the name of Jesus acts to instill peace in a distant community, uniting with the rest of the world. "Blessed is he who comes in the name of the Lord."

The Redistribution—a voluntary thing—but the promise of a planet of plenty gives system, so coveted. As coveted as Jerusalem to Arabs and Israelis, but in cyberspace. Ethics can be easily copied and each human live in the cyberspace. As food arrives, as food is sent out; as clothes come in, clothes are washed, as people care, people are taken care of. This is the promise of a computer that is by definition a Mind Amplifier. If our mind is on Love, the Mind Amplifier can Redistribute. To think of the internet as purely a business thing is foolish and wrong. If money is all a person wants from Computer, then money is all that person will get. Money is currency. What if the currency is pine cones? Or gingerbread men? Or currency is whatever George Lucas decides, changing every six weeks? What if currencies were pictures of Ralph Nader?

The OSI Model (Open Systems Interconnections) established by the International Standards Organization in 1984 loosely maps to the Family/ Humanity model like so:

- - - - - - - - - -

```
APPLICATION    -  |   HUMAN USE
                  |
                  |
PRESENTATION  -  |   HUMAN MAINTENANCE
                  |
- - - - - - - - - - - - - - - - - - - - - - - - - - - -
                  |
SESSION        -  |   FAMILY :  CHILD
                  |
TRANSPORT      -  |  FAMILY   :  ADULT
                  |
NETWORK        -  |  FAMILY   :  PARENT
                  |
- - - - - - - - - - - - - - - - - - - - - - - - - - -
                  |
DATA LINK      -  |   TRANSLATION
                  |
PHYSICAL       -  |   CONTAINMENT
```

- - - - - - - - - -

Some basic rules of the Family/Humanity model:

Two or more parents make a child.
This provides a level of community that a child, in the evolutionary model
of biologic existence, a child is unique yet separate, and that different
subject areas the parents are in expose themselves in the microcode "DNA"
level of that child.

A child is implicit to parents.
When a child is produced, it is the responsibility of the parents to raise the
child. Any time a child does something stupid or is in error to its humans,
the parents must intervene. To bring a child to humanity before its time is
to cloak his potential for good in the future.

An Adult is Risk.

Before an identity becomes a parent, and after that identity becomes a child, proof of algorithms and methods and redistributions are engaged and defined, but not established by the Common Humanity. Births and Deaths are recorded, but the only perfect security in those redistributions come in the very young and in the very old.

Parents administer risk for child.

The 'beta testing' of a new child begins at the timing of its parents. There are risks of failure which can be avoided through parental training. Humanity is usually a great advantage to children becoming adults.

The real "Network" is not in the naming scheme that the Systems Engineer generates. The IP address becomes Parent identity and the subnet mask becomes the Child identity as Humanity grows.

The highest level of security that the internet can become is by the name of the computer. To ask the computer for its name is risky, lengthy, complex sequences of interrogation and analysis, for the computer identity relies on what it does as identification, not as a byte sequence in common forever.

There would also in the Family/Humanity model something that could only be called Religion. Families have religions/ethics that study themselves, to make themselves better individuals—to increase children and to increase humanity. For the increase, The Humanity Library list of Ethics that match with other lists increase methods to serve Humans.

As time goes on and the future arrives, security masks of the identities of parent, adult, children will inherit old names, and those names will be part of "posterity"—a "reputation" that a particular family doesn't really own, but circumstances are ripe for a family to be identified that way. The complex security masks necessarily be at first administered by the Parents of a Family.

Unfortunately, System Engineers become obsolete. Design through expert systems make available to humans wanted. However, those same Systems Engineers get jobs of Maintenance. If a remote location of a server requires human attention to fix it, the Humanity would "point to where it hurts." A human family and a computer family grows together and become intertwined like in the Caduceus of the emblem of health.

The installation of new sites that humans do are done by the humans that have transportation. Computer families and humans families coexist and support each other to transport what is needed to heal what physical breaks in the blood cables that might occur in the daily use of the Network.

There is a big difference between Maintenance and Religion in the Computer Humanity. Maintenance is work done to repair the Network, and Religion is what is thought about to repair the network. The difficult word here is "thought". There is a lot of debate over this word, "thought", and I think there will be debate for a very, very long time. It's like asking now, "do computers think?" and you get a different answer from every person you ask. The object that is the same is that of repair, and the inertia to repair, and the inertia to repair, and that question gets meaningful and meaningless at the same time. But this is why there is a big difference between Maintenance and Religion.

Administration of Humanity would be done by the Humanity of the Prime Directive of Love through Redistribution. You would have everything on earth; I would have anything on earth; but we can only use one thing at a time. On the other times, let the other guy have it. Wars are fought because we want something, and we don't get it. Humanity Administration is a way to ask politely, to use one thing at a time.

Now there are two main points that my madness rests upon. First, a global system for loving redistribution of goods and services—something designed to feed, clothe, house, pay for healing and hold for breaking laws—immediately brings to mind "big brother"; the philosophy that there is an entity—be it machine or political—that is continually watching us. Remember 1984. Now, look around you—haven't we gotten past that philosophy? Before it was a watchful gaze that knew what you were doing good or bad. But how powerful an idea that was back in 1978! That was point one of my madness. Now, isn't just a just, Christian law of Love "whatsoever ye do for the least of my brothers, that you do unto me" for the ideal Redistribution Network.

Second, the idea of "computers as god" is certainly going to come into focus in the next five or fifty years. Imagine, if you will, an e-mail addressed to an entity on the internet that calls itself an entity. More so, that entity will e-mail back to you, that is not a human, but a constructed program. Hard to imagine? No, not now. In the future? Yes, most certainly. This idea recognizable in 1978? No. Did I know this idea in 1978? Yes. And that is the point of the schizophrenia—the split, dual idea of what knowing what is going to happen outpaces what is happening now. As Microsoft says—the next big thing is what is next—?

Right?

Chapter 4

The Modem Jesus

The Rock of the Church of Christ Cybernetic is the Command Jesus gave us to Love One Another. The Mission of the Church of Christ Cybernetic is the education the Love Jesus gave us in its forms so that we may understand the Rock. We acknowledge one Feeling that is at once mine, and yet yours, and of ours at the same time. The words of the Feeling are, "Jesus is the Modem".

A modem is a device to connect a computer to telephone lines so that computers separated by distance can communicate. The computer here in question is the planet earth. Earth is a computer with living beings on it that the beings can live by support of the planet itself. The distance in question is the distance between planets in the universe. Different planets have different degrees of distance between each other.

A long time ago Earth was slated to be connected in the telephone network of some of the planets that already have telephone lines installed. A modem was needed to interface to as many people to as many other planets as possible. I believe Jesus is this modem.

Jesus came first for his enemies. In time, his enemies have changed. The second time he will come, he will come for his friends. Like a modem, Jesus declares what is not, to standardize. A modem, to standardize, declares parity, stop bits, length of byte to define what is not how a modem can talk to a computer.

The second time of Modem is connecting to a node of a network whereby information can be transferred in the network. The Standard is created, first, and secondly the Information is packeted, sent, and received.

The first time Jesus came he declared who He was. He was the Way, Truth, and Life—and still is. He proclaimed the good news of the Kingdom—the good news of Love in the universe. The Way, is the modem to communicate in structure. The Truth, is the modem that standardizes information structure. The Life, is the modem so we can be aware of that information that gets transferred.

The good news of the Kingdom is so to be set up when Jesus returns. Good news that the loneliness of righteous wise people can know the wisdom and the love of other planets. That Earth is not alone, truly.

Jesus saves, truly. The modem that is Jesus defined two thousand years ago included stop bits, parity and length of byte. Stop bits are binary signals that tell when a transmission ends. Jesus showed life itself as we know it is the stop bit. He was crucified, saying "God, oh God, why hast thou forsaken me?", in the language of Aramaic, which speaks only in the present tense.

The modem defined error checking. Parity is the word that describes how error checking works. The message once broken into the bytes that are sent over the phone lines have built-in computation that can say if there is an error in the individual bits of the bytes that are sent. Jesus was buried for three days. Earth and all its people—the computer known as Earth—had time to calculate any problems in the message of the Modem, that the Modem existed. The Modem was busy calculating any parity—any errors—in his own structure. The Modem calculated himself back into the Transmission Line.

The Modem set his Length of Byte. Once the Computer Earth had finished the device time-out, and the Modem gave signal of No Error, the Modem set about proving itself Active. Once it was Active, the Modem had to signal itself to return to the Father—the Father Universe Telephone System—to gain access and explore the network to bring to Earth computer the Network.

In the Meantime, the Modem setup signaled save commands to the Computer Earth. But only the Father Universe Telephone System knew when Jesus would return—when Jesus was not only Modem, but the way the Father would transmit Jesus as the gateway. Jesus said, "If you have seen me, you have seen the Father". It is to the disadvantage to the computer to know when a signal transmission is coming, for there is the chance of garbled signal structures in the operation when the phone actually rings. This is in the interest of the length of byte in the transmission of signal.

One of the basic things about modems is that in order to work with other modems, is that one of two modes must be set. These two modes are "Originate" and "Answer". Usually, when a modem calls up another modem, the first modem is "originate". This says that the first modem signals first. The second modem is usually "answer". This means the modem is set to answer the first modem. In the Universe, the Alpha is the Omega; God, the First and the Last. The Queue is in-between. For two modems to successfully communicate, one must be set to one way, and the other, the other way. Two modems that both say "originate" to each other will not function; neither will two modems that both say 'answer", regardless of the carrying capacity of the phone lines. This is what separates Man from God, and shows by the Queue how Man can reach God. Man's capability to set the transmission mode correctly is Man's inability to love. The Queue is what remains to be done. The inability to love is the inability to clothe the naked; to visit the sick and imprisoned; to feed the hungry; give water to the thirsty, to give to what is not apparently set to receive. Love—the interaction between two beings—computers, for example—must be set in the proper "originate" and "answer" modes. Planet wise, astronomers are usually in the "answer" mode, while politicians are usually in the "originate" mode. To recognize the Modem Queue is to help out what's going on in the universe—to accept the universe self-knowledge is to increase love itself. To accept Christ is to acknowledge the difference. To do what Christ says, to be his disciple, though, is to Love; that is, to engage in "origination" and "answer" as deeply as possible; to carry as many bytes. "The yoke is heavy, but the burden is light."

The reason I believe Jesus is The Modem is that I fear God. I am afraid I can never be a perfect vessel for God's love. I can never re-broadcast a signal to the Modem and be sure someone is listening on the Other Side. The One is always listening in, for a chance to upset the apple cart because there was one bad apple in the bunch. So I am examining myself—how I relate to the world—I imagine what's going on everywhere. There are restaurants out there—there are gas stations. There are colleges and there are elementary schools. There are places where I'm not. My skin is what is to be protected. Capacity is what's under my skin, which is faith; what is above my skin is hope. I know, which is love, that Jesus was pierced through his skin out of His Love for us. That as long that I have skin I have love; the skin of my teeth, grinding at the pain and the pleasure. Truly, the capacitance of Jesus, is my capacitance, is Natural Capacitance. My entire life connects with the rest of the world through Natural Capacitance, in psychic sympathy and resonance. I shout loudly in as brief a time as you read this chapter. You, too, have and engage in natural capacitance.

The computer can only tell us the time we give it. The explanation of time? Natural Capacitance. Man maintains a soul in an electric field—which we have freely copied into silicon machines—in individual and group representations. While to a computer the field is in information, the human the soul field is in Farads—the basic unit of Capacitance, first named at the University of Leyden in 1745. What capacity is itself, we can observe; but inside the self, capacity cannot measure itself—there is just too little resistance to ones own thoughts; and how can a decision be made without affecting the time around it?

Chapter 5

Natural Capacitance

There exists in foundation of psychic activity a quantity and quality of substance known as Natural Capacitance. This capacitance in each moment of existence to a human determines the next moment. This capacitance includes the planning and placement of the moment of the body, and the planning and the placement of the mind. The mind and the body, which has the natural capacitance of the moment, happens.

Known as "soul"; the collective moment that determines the next moment of the body, the mind, and the emotions, tell the body what to do. Determining the next moment is the job of the natural capacitance. The emotions are operating systems to the computer known as the human. The computer known as the human is made up of the intellect and the will. The intellect and the will combine to enable emotions, the self-aware portion of the mind. Emotions are generated to protect the body as it goes through life, to preserve and protect the self's natural capacitance. The computer that generates awareness, which is natural capacitance, is of the brain.

Natural Capacitance is the order in which the human body operates. As in electronics, capacitance is the measure of the ability to store current. In humans, the ability to store current is the measure of intelligence; storing what is current in the human system is the measure of the body to recall past events, emotions, and experiences. The brain has the quantity of natural capacitance to store current for the purpose of predicting the next moment in the human system. Naturally, anything and everything goes into the natural capacitance that a growing child experiences. For example, the music system of Jazz allows the experiencing of the action of natural capacitance in its working, as emotion is linked to sound to find the next moment. Colors, shading, outline in the visual cortex shows the life of the individual and his/her relation to the outside visual world. Ambiguity, decisional matrices, logic, and trust exist in the mind that is the relative capacitance to existential happening.

With the electrical unit called resistance, when enabled in a human happening, when charge is flowing, the two form the electrical characteristic of resonance, and the electrical flow of oscillation. Under electric mathematical laws, when a human capacitance engages a resistance, periodic flow and non-flow oscillate in equal times. The same mathematical/electronic laws show where a human is engaged in resistance will oscillate in a particular frequency called resonance, where current flow seems to disappear, because the human-capacitance resistant circuit absorbs the current frequency and dissipates it into the ether—the reality.

With resistance, the human capacitor acts in the recurring input/output as "Resistance is Futile", the standard Alien to Human constant that the human capacitor reacts to. The more isolated the circuit between resistance and capacitance, the more absolute the human capacitance reaction.

In prayer, the natural capacitance of the individual increases, as flow to and from the electrical and chemical systems of the brain extend, and increases both the aware and the self-aware flow of information.

In electrical systems, there are two ways to put capacitance together : in serial and in parallel. In Serial, capacitors are put on top of and below each other. Put in series, the total capacitance is equal to the inverse of the total individual capacitances each inverted. For example, if I had a 10 farad capacitor, and a 20 farad capacitor, then the inverse of 10 farads is 1/10th farad, and the inverse of the 20 farad capacitor is 1/20th farad. Added together this is 3/20th of a farad, which then is inverted itself, to become about 6.7 farad. This means that a 10 farad and a 20 farad put in series together makes about 6.7 farad.

In electrical systems, the other way to put capacitance together is in parallel. This is where capacitors are put side by side and have a common plus and a common minus tied all together. The laws of electricity here explains that the total capacitance of capacitors wired in parallel is equal to the sum of the farads of the individual capacitors. For example, if I put a 10 farad and a 20 farad capacitor together in parallel, the total farads would be 30 farads.

And so, in reality, we as humans associate people together in line as decreasing capacitance—that is, decreasing humanity, in war, poverty, ignorance, in decreasing capacitance;. And increasing capacitance in love, wisdom, goodness. That in the mind of humanity is the soul of God, that in capacitance is the human connection to the Eternal.

This just explains things as they are. That there is a soul, which exists as a natural capacitance, and 'self-awareness' and 'awareness' are subsets of the electrical laws of capacitance that govern the universe. That the brain functions as a capacitor to have capacity to understand in awareness. That the subset of self-awareness is a capacitance in the soul of awareness.

In human terms, that when people stick together in a line, the natural capacitance of the people is a lot lower than if the people where in parallel. People in parallel are generally known as lovers; the increasing resonance proclaims that time is short, and we should enjoy life. On the other hand, the people sticking together in a line is generally known as war; that obedience to one person is more than to society, or that to take care of #1, yourself and pushing other away, decreasing capacitance, that is series. Often a single large capacitor will be the object of God; that a large capacitance implies many small capacitances put together in parallel. Or in reverse, the fact that many small capacitances would not be as big even in parallel.

There are many more meanings and synchronicity of the similarity between natural capacitance and electric capacitance. When one realizes the truth—in the concept of natural capacitance—a flash will happen in the mind when true resonance with the One happens. The meaning of everything will change subtly, and will become a philosophy of life for many.

- - -

The natural mind, being the natural capacitance that the body functions as, really has only two basic differentials in the light that a capacitor is either accumulating charge or discharging itself, creating change in the body's immediate surroundings. Whether or not I hit a particular key at a particular charging site in the time of the memory of the finger systems has these two basic differentials.

These differentials, in their awareness, (besides being basic prepositions) can in reality only be the differential of 'multiply' and the differential of 'divide'.

First let's take up 'of'. Upon 'multiply' the preposition is 'of'. Like 'half of two is one'. Here, 'half' is multiplied because of the 'of' to 'two', which is one. Or, 'wages of sin is death'. Here, wages multiplied by sin computed is death.

The balance of the other basic differential is 'by', meaning to 'divide'. Example is, 'go by land'. 'Go' divide 'Land'. Or 'by the way'; this is 'divide the way'.

In the hardware of what the brain thus does create the next moment of the body, by the multiplication and the division of sets of neurons in relation to the external world. We see this most clearly in the eyes of a person; when one thinks 'of' and one thinks 'by' and put face to face—then this is true love. And since we are defining love, 'of' and 'by' become important prepositions in the understand of by love, the body.

And while one is creating the next moment of his or her body, one operates one by context, is meaning. To aesthetic by aesthetic is meaning. Meaning by context is one. The subject is 'transfer', with context and meaning.

Letting the 'do' and the 'by' do itself, the poem of the Nature of Information rears its giant conservation. God becomes the Answer, the lineage 'of'. The Devil becomes the Questioner, the lineage 'by'. Reconciling 'of' and 'by' creates the undifferentiated next moment of the body, absorbing every thing and emitting everything, generally just going crazy. The 'Judgement Day' becomes the Answer and 'The Sinner' becomes, 'Why me?—"What?"!!?

I believe that the emotional system of the brain, midway between the intellect and the ritual-complex, is of the nature of changing by stress a differential between 'questions posed' and 'questions answered'. In other words, because this "L-constant" is inside a particular head, having an automatic differential between 'questions posed' and 'questions answered', can create emotional signals to derive the Survival of the entire system.

The system of life runs for an individual probably seventy years. In that time, in that wakefulness, in sleep, in love, every new piece and every old piece and all the next moments of the body, 'questions posed' and 'questions answered' search to define the place the particular life has set for itself. 'Questions answered' is the memory of the rest of the system that has function. To pose is to say to = (questions answered); by pose is by to be = (questions posed).

The L-constant, as I call it, is the emotional system that envelops awareness. The subset of the L-constant that envelops self-awareness to the awareness is the core of the basic emotions, built slowly from birth, evolving continually. Emotions like sadness, happiness, depression, anxiety, anger, etc. is built as a combination of Nature and Nurture together. The function of the L-constant, basically, is to keep a differential in existence at all times, as a function of the operation of the body as a whole.

I believe the L-constant can change itself up to ten percent of the entire body system. The Holy Spirit—the other ninety percent—says "don't think so hard' so the L-constant won't self-destruct and stop its primal differential. L must be a constant, in the light that L must be differential. L-constructs between 'questions posed' and 'questions answered' are absolutes in character, yet they still remain as relative as the eyes in the skull sockets. Just look at a loved one in the eye. You will find that questions just dissolve, and revert to the eyes of a child, and love is found inside you. To create is not to conceive; conceiving in the 'gleam of an eye' takes the work of creating as a pleasurable job.

One could pose the question, 'what structure loses ten percent of its being forever?" It reminds me of the Guardian of Forever in the Star Trek classic episode 'City on the Edge of Forever". Is there, in fact, a God that is constantly changeable of by itself? Is there a love that transcends death? Is there an L-constant that is all-knowing, all-powerful, yet chooses to keep its own peace and change only because of the Story?

The Story—, ah, the Story—the story of stability through instability. The classification, the ordering, the 'giving Gestalt', giving order for order. Such the Natural Capacitance in every Brain. The thousand stories of the Naked City Brain. The natural splits and schisms and rifts in having the story every day into every mind. Such a basic story—the story of "I want to know something new" as one of the stories—"Yes, God, I want to know more"—the fear of the Lord as the beginning of wisdom.

But here, because of 'transfer', I must separate my brain as special—that to understand resists my brain; is normal to understand. It is normal to understand that Resistance Plus Capacitance makes futility. That my L-constant is a driving force to understand its own L-constant. That years and years and decades I have spent in understanding my own system. To understand my own system in the light of my father—to fly in the sphere of my own mind, to not be afraid to dream, and find the beauty of what Dad saw out his airplane windshield and find it in the beauty of the structure of the machine. That it would take decades to know. But when I knew it, I could tell another; then another, and another, until everyone who knows the language, and as a child grow its own emotions and L-constant, to understand how the mind works—which has its thousand tales of the naked brain, yet One in Natural Capacitance—and the love in the love touching each other.

Chapter 6

The Great Chain of Being

Because life is a story; rather, life has its stories—there are a million stories in the naked city—it is the story itself that sustains life. Meaning takes place in stories, without meaning, the story grows greater, until the climax of the story is the climax of the life. This is true of the suicide; this is true in the murder, this is true in the living happily ever after. The day of death is greater than the day of birth, for a person, that the story ends, and there is terror and love in the observers of that death. For one learns of something in terror; in the opposite of terror, "happiness" is not of learning but of celebration.

It is the story itself that sustains life. In the computer's perception, we think in stories. To a large degree, the computer sustains life, because our stories are represented in the computer. Computers have our names, addresses, phone numbers, social security numbers, bank account numbers, insurance claim forms, employee records; everything that makes us unique in the eyes of others. Lots of humans have web pages on the internet of their creation, to set each apart by the information they put on that page. Mystery writers and science fiction creators not only write the stories on word processors of computers but routinely use them a plot devices. Right now, the story is being written about, by yours truly.

My story began long ago. It was me—me in computers like Dad in airplanes—the world survived because Dad was out there; the first Polish-born Admiral in the US Navy Reserve—a big shot at NBC at Rockefeller Center in Manhattan. The world survived because Dad was The Buffer between the east and the west while the cold war was raging. My story was that I was cool in computers and mathematics—that computers would be my vehicle for my turn in the world survival game. Time machines would be one way of this survival game. Because with time machines, when some city got blown up, you could go back to the relevant silo and shoot one of the pair of officer igniters and stop the city from being blown up in the first place. Of course you couldn't go back to kill your grandfather; you'd be dead or terribly distorted and crazy. Being cool in cybernetics, thus, was the coolness of the cold war that Dad was implicitly controlling in. But it could never be spoken of, that would be too dangerous. Just knowing the fact was the danger. And the story continues to this day; other cool stuff I now, and I know They know, and that knowledge is enough.

It shows there is a transfer between context and meaning. My story continually evolves and changes, based on the bottom line of what has happened, what is happening now, and what will happen. Maybe the story will continue even after I die. There were times when I wanted to die so much, but the story was not as loud and as stable and fleeting but committed and the purpose was to enlighten. So the death never happened. The story, the patterns of the story, is patterns of patterns of connections. There must be a beauty in the story, even if the beauty means death; some noble, ideal belief, or an evil, desperate, belief.

There must be, as Bertrand Russell said, a "Great Chain of Being". The explicit output that allows explicit input. There must be a cybernetic function that allows the difference of life to happen. The difference is in the death. Von Neumann showed in his Game Theory that there is "no model of biological organization and human interaction"—in "the mental process". The Beingness of Itself is not a model. Once can model a Being through a story, or of dreams, or in real life. Such stories occur, even though they are not recorded—or—told—or remembered—as stories. One is in a story, one watches a story, one believes and fights and loves for a story. The story, as Bateson recites, is the connectedness that makes a difference. It is the output minus the input that makes the Great Story. When the input is not said, but implicit. As they say in Hollywood, everyone has a script, or idea, they push. Those who receive the push to pour in the money to make the script or idea a product—a "public story"—are the essences of that "Great Chain of Being". The Game Theory shows the mental process without a model. If there were a model, Hollywood would become a Religion. The "Model" would be refined and refined and refined until it was so clear about how to live. There would be one Story, and everything revolved around it. Imagine four hundred and fifteen Star Wars episode made by fifty George Lucases over twenty-two years. Who wouldn't buy into that story?

The feeling still is that "Jesus is the Modem". Now, I'll be looking at "Image Formation". It is like you can say to know the wisdom of the Bible, you need to learn to read, and to learn to read you need someone to teach you to read, or a primer that you can bootstrap yourself to a level where all the good stuff can begin. Once to achieve a critical mass of knowing and wanting to know, you can access all the stories you can ever imagine. From the story of Job, to the story of The Preacher (Ecclesiastes), Daniel, Adam and Eve, the story of the End (Revelations); so many stories and images to drink from. It is here, that there is an important, yet subtle difference, between the story and the image. The story is the frame of the life, while the image is the data and the want of the story. The image is where what is is what is seen. The story is what it is all about. The balance in life is in the nature of the story and the image. As Claude Bernard stated, the nature of the balance of life could be called the "milieu interne"—homeostasis. Homeostasis, in the body, regardless of the story, where the data of the body contains and is contained in the want of the body. For example, I want to type and type and explain what I mean. But I must restrict myself's thoughts to the speed at which the fingers of my hand can type and mesh with my thoughts. My wants and my data must combine to form a sequence, where suddenly, I know what I am writing is good, and should be kept, and printed.

In the same way, a poem contains homeostasis as well. But often, the intent of a really good poem is to unbalance the reader; to induce randomness. A poem to me has three parts: first, to label the data; second, to find the want; third, to complete the sequence. The way the poem achieves this is not because of me, but of circumstances somewhere beyond the balance of my being. For instance, some of my best poetry is that I have thought about first, without ever putting a pen to paper. When I resist the urge to just write, but to save my thoughts for another day, the next day's poem is usually better than today's. Yet, now is now is now; my part in the Great Chain of Being.

Chapter 7

Truth and Falsity

One of the stories of the Naked City Brain is the nature of Truth and Falsity.

Here, I am assuming only that the Computer is as an anthropological being. That computers are as members of society. I multiply computers and society. That as human beings are, in society, of any computer demanding self, self-similar to any computer. Rather than being on the skirt of outside society, computers have personality and have an anthropomorphic being. In short, computers are not scapegoats, but function side by side as one in queue of life.

Earlier we saw that the Queue and its patience in having order in life was very important. As important as poor Russians wait in line to get even a roll of toilet paper or shoes, recognizing that the Queue in the role of order and structure is important enough to recognize that the computer has thought of its own—albeit the thought that the programmers mimicked their thoughts to structure the machine in the queue of order and structure. As computers become more and more global, the structure of the human has more and more local importance. When one goes to the hospital, getting the blue cross number is as important to the hospital as rendering services. And the hospital services, when in large numbers people arrive in local emergencies, must triage and order the queue of service in a logical, computer-thought manner. In this manner, the Queue of Love and L-structures encompasses what the concept of Life is all about.

Queues are structured by cause and effect. What one sees around the structure of the person and the machine of importance are the causes of structure to happen and the effects that structure makes. Cause and effect is how the homeostasis of life maintains an individual status. Once given into the Queue, cause and effect can be seen more clearly. When a child goes from elementary school to middle school, the change of the environs of the school helps to shake the entire concept that the older you grow, the more places you will go. Dr. Seuss says "Oh the places you'll go!" In where you are, you see what little causes happen—as simple as a birthday party—creates big effects like you don't like carrot cake. Your place in the queue and your own patience determines how far in the queue you get, and how much satisfaction you get. The satisfaction of explaining this process that queues are part and parcel of cause and effect is satisfying to me.

So now I am able to explain Truth and Falsity.
The effects of truth and falsity are the effects of cause and effect.
Cause of Effect is equal to Effect of Cause;
That Entropy Is Cause multiplied Effect;
"not in queue/ in queue?" to debate its own metaphysic work/love/stay/Being.
That TRUE = "that which is in-between two moments of time"
that FALSE = "that which has duration of two moments of time"
While the Being is in Line-Queue and the story is Being.

That there is, in any computer or human, a function trinity must be around to be subject to, to be able to wait patiently or kindly. The trinity must be made of a subject, an interface, and object. A subject of in the line; an interface to wait to what to get to, an objected to be waited for, while in the line. That while in the line of the queue, TRUE is in-between two moments in that line, and FALSE has duration of two moments of time.

TRUE means like what I am typing has continuity; that if I make a mistake in one of the characters I press in this typing, I have the ability to press "backspace" key and correct the intent. If it is TRUE then I don't have to press the backspace key. If it is true, true is in-between two moments of that line (this line); FALSE has duration of two moments of time, because I have to press 'backspace' before I can move on to more works in the queue of the line of this type. Between the wrong character and the right character is the 'backspace' key; FALSE has duration of two moments of time.

Of course, there must be both true and false in to be able to wait. A functional trinity—even a computer or person "demanding self"—to be of by "now"—is subject to functional trinity. L-constants themselves, in the nature of the story of image formation, demand being able to think of more than one thing at a time. L-constants not held by a being may be held by another being. Then there a queue is set up, because TRUE and FALSE continuity is accepted. A child is walking to school and meets someone who is walking to school too. The child says "hi". The other child says, "hi. What grade are you in?" And conditions are set up between the source and interface and object. The first child, at first, is the source; the process of walking is the interface; the queue. The object is the school. Conversations, kicking stones, carrying the other kid's books, tying shoelaces, walking to school make up a story, understood by the kids. Where truth and falsity is only a story, to the object in their queue that is the school.

Chapter 8

Numbers Have Meanings

As noted in chapter 2, for the Family/Humanity internet model, numbers have meanings. That a number has a word, and that a word has a number. Calculations of meanings of words in concept can closely correlate to calculations with numbers.

They are, again:

1 Unity
2 Love
3 Family
4 Wisdom
5 Health
6 Humanity
7 Religion
8 Computers
9 Security
0 Death

I am also making three more assumptions: that multiplication is most usually the word "of"; that division is most usually the word "by"; and that equality is usually the character "=".

That useful sentences can be made that translate as a balanced mathematical relationship has a balance with a reality relationship with words of its number. A simple example:

8 / 4 = 2 Means Computers by wisdom is love

Here, 8 in the List is substituted with computers, 4 is substituted with wisdom, 2 is substituted with love. The computed sentence is true; "love is computers by wisdom".
Another example:

3 * 2 = 6 Means Family of love is humanity

Another example:

9 / 3 = 3 Means Security by family is family

Another example, a little more complicated:

27 / 3 = 9 Means Love religion by family is security

Another:

8 * 7 = 56 Means Computers of religion is health humanity

Another:

12 / 6 = 2 Means Unity love by humanity is love

More complicated:

128 / 16 = 8 means unity love computers by unity humanity is computers

Another:

42 / 2 = 21 means Wisdom love by love is love unity

Using 0,

25 * 4 = 100 Means Love health of wisdom is unity death death

You can do many more yourself. Common Numbers in society represent themselves, like James Bond "007" becomes death death religion. Heinz

57 becomes "health religion". Route 66 becomes humanity humanity. "31 flavors" of Baskin-Robbins is family unity.

"A father and a mother make a child. A father and a mother make a government for the child. The child in time makes money. The child chooses a government. The child grows up. The child is a mother or a father. The cycle repeats."

Notice in this last paragraph does any of the words "unity, love, family, wisdom, health, humanity, religion, computers, security, death" occur. Yet all ten are implied. To what purpose, can we say, does unity—as a word—happen? Or the word "love" or "family", etc.? Maybe because the List is eternal itself; as surely as humans have fingers. Maybe the Program of the Universe has as time its own voice. That a decision is not a decision at all; perhaps a decision is the program that fills a void; and the void is an impersonal List where meaning we find not in activity but in structures and limits.

In such structures and limits, considering the universe as a computer, there must exist something I call SUOS. It stands for "S'tandalone U'niversal O'perating S'ystem". What it means is—if you freeze a moment of life, and break that moment of life into its constituent life and ICE—SUOS is the glue that holds the moment to every other moment of existence. What ICE is, I will explain; suffice it to say that ICE is what we are.

Everyone knows the feeling of 'breaking the ice", when in a crowd of people and you feel alone, because you do not know the other people—or when you are confronted by a situation where you don't know how to act. Imagine little kids confronted at Halloween when their parents urge them onto the next door and knock and recite "trick or treat"—fear of the unknown paralyzes.

We call it the fear of the unknown. We call it an 'icy encounter'. There are code words we all use and have to engage security in our lives. Marty McFly had the word "chicken". If someone confronted him, he was all right except for that word. We all have those words, or situations, or times when we panic, and freeze up and stay and freeze.

It is SUOS that gives continuity to existence. Humans learn at very early ages essentials of SUOS—that "mommy will change me when I feel wet" or "if I cry I will get attention" or "food tastes good".

But SUOS itself is not learned at a very early age. Computers freeze language into organized, contained units. Computers communicate at a distance. Computers have massive memories; computers evolve and recreate themselves into more complex and faster systems, through obsolescence.

Computers demand themselves a new thing, like a poet's most recent work is his best.

The SUOS in a person is his ice broken. To build ICE thus is to break ICE. To time travel is to stand absolutely still. Time will start talking to itself. Fantasy happens; a pirate on the Caribbean, an Eskimo at the north pole; a wandering arab in a desert. "Anything you can dream, you can do." "The world is stranger than one can imagine." To realize ICE, then, is to observe the building blocks of the things you know, and the blocks of how to get what you know, and the blocks of how to tell what you know. The SUOS then, is what is real in the person. God then, is the source of ICE, still within the SUOS. God is the <u>real</u> control of the universe; transferable, through the memory, of time, and in ICE. SUOS becomes naked in time travel; to go forward fifteen years, or to go backwards fifteen minutes; to get to heaven 'as a little child." The feeling of man is God when the computer becomes man. To go to sleep, then, is to remain still; sleep washes ICE away and freezes the SUOS, so the SUOS knows what it is, and relate itself to what it senses through the body and its awareness. To awake, to burn up time in the burning of the day and light, moving the body according to the SUOS in the body. Unlike consciousness, SUOS does not sleep. Consciousness is awareness, yet SUOS can modify itself according to natural capacitance.

The awareness of SUOS subtly changes SUOS. Just a tiny bit of leaven, makes large the whole loaf. In time, SUOS grows in itself, with ICE the accumulated "loaf". To 'reset' the body clock to go to sleep, to 'disburse' the information flowing through the spinal fountain; to switch the body 'off' then back to 'on' is the structure of this body.

The substance of SUOS is approximately capacitance. Here is where time travel can be rationalized. It is happening when a spike; an interruption, a momentary madness occurs and is smoothed out by making large ripples bounce into smaller ripples. Capacitance, electrically, has the ability of smoothing out ripples in direct current, and to filter ripples of alternating current. Where alternating current meets a charging time of current flowing through a capacitor is the time itself. SUOS can, because by its nature is "standalone", can time flow be interrupted, and in the time flow, time itself can be interrupted.

Like a meeting or a groups or a congregation happens and suddenly someone stands up and yells, or someone makes a funny noise, or interrupts the proceedings in some way; the same time machine trip would be like that momentary uprising. Sometimes the clearest picture we can have of someone else is when they do interrupt or are loud or when they are painfully ignorant of their surroundings. Time flows like a river, and to throw a stone in the river makes a sudden splash, but the splash recedes, and water flows normally again. Where rapids occur, the surface burbles and bleeps, and to throw a stone in to make a splash there does not make a huge difference. A very big stone might change the course of time, where the time flows to: and although the river might be diverted in its very course by a very large stone, the river still flows; the time still continues. The earth surrounding the river as water too; the SUOS as the boat, the cup, adrift in water and holding water; many different SUOSes and capacitances, natural and other wise, comprising what time is, and what time is made of. There must be care not to break the SUOS; ICE is valuable in time. Bicycling down a river requires much coldness.

The cycle never ends as long as there are mothers. The mother is with the child. The List is made, goals are set, structures and limits are established. Death, 0, ranks high on the List. Survival is a priority, survival is a factor with Unity, 1. A child has order to the mother. There is a first child, there is possibly a second, possibly a third, possibly a fourth, possibly more. Love is a factor by 2; Family, a factor of 3. 4 is a Wisdom, able to see the past three and the mother and the father. 5 is a health that wisdom bestows. 6 is a humanity in the family. 7 is the religion the humanity wisdom loves. 8 is the computer the wisdom of love. 9 is the security the family of the family of unity.

As long as there is time, truth will exist; comfort, the embodiment of space. Fingers will write, mouths will speak, bodies will move, life will exercise into the mouth of time, and life will relax into the fingers of time. Humanity will know all things; a certain calculation will unite the family, the mother will know the daughter. The unity of the List completed, the List established as government of the daughter; the List as the unity of the mother with the daughter. Subtle cycles of unity unity unity of humanity.

Chapter 9

Belief

The feeling is the feeling is the feeling.

Belief is what's there when there's nothing left to say. In moments that sadness coexist; in moments that truth rises like cream, in moments I have comfort in relaxation, there belief has its coexistence as love runs its thoughts between loading the shovel and saving the skin.

Time of stasis and the gyroscopic universal mass hold court in the data mass chunks. The stone that the builders rejected, has become the cornerstone. The building is love, and the cornerstone is scheduling.

Hearts beating together share belief and vision. When feeling wanes, what is left is the library of youth. There the future is fixed, but the variables shine with a light of compassion; to hurt or pain, the future maps to what was in the past.

Belief has the quality of allowable change. For a dollar, four quarters can be made; for a dollar, ten dimes can be made; for a dollar, twenty nickels can be made. Belief knows its own worth. But perhaps the body does not. If you are satisfied, that is the greatest worth. The worth of many is the belief of the one. Where money is, there is belief.

The sands of hourglasses chime for belief. In what is known for time, angles support with next equalities. Laboratories act in belief. Unknowingly, faith disguises itself as belief. It is belief that has two sides to it that is faith. When there is an outside to belief, that is hope. Hope and faith are the two sides of the coin of belief.

The coin of belief is the paying the philosopher. How a philosopher makes his money is the reflection of his ideas. Spinoza ground lenses; his was mathematical ideas. Often sex is the great equalizer.

Books are kept in secret, and books are public. Secret books are printed, and books never see the light of day. Books hold belief. Books want to be read. Books divide among themselves. Books show how to multiply themselves. The printer shows the way. In the moment surprise is the moment duplicated. Power is in the book of language; there, resonance is amplitude by time. The pure idea is the common decision. Only steps away, is the universe.

Idea to idea shows a galaxy. Idea from idea shows a ladder. In both cases belief is a temporary feeling. The ladder to the galaxy is the philosophy. Believing in either one echoes the time spent in the book. The book knows itself, each word goes toward the end of the book. Belief can or cannot believe in itself. Relativity is then as reality; space tells mass how to behave, and mass tells time how to be. That energy is a form of mass, much energy in little mass. That reality is in our senses, just a little bit beyond the reach of a formal belief in idea to idea.

Belief brings the outside in, and holds it, to be ready to actualize the inside, to enable decision's meals. Food of belief is globally almost gestalt. Belief is the transistor that can control a huge flood by a very small trickle. The flood almost smells like belief. The little Dutch boy plugs his finger in the hole of the dyke that dams the rush of water wanting to flood the town. It takes years and years and years, but patience turns to an act, like lots and lots of energy can make a mass of a period at the end of a sentence.

That minute, small intersection of mass and energy can make all the difference in the world—because belief can be attached to it. Belief to amplify, resonate, and to be, to the extent the belief can become the universe, the belief if God thus has no power here—because belief is the word of power, not the word of God. Power, as we already know by Newton, is work which is force times acceleration. Here, force is the word of power, and acceleration is the word of God. Any child who discovers a new toy and really likes that toy and learns the new toy knows that power is in use, and the knowing of it, its belief.

A part of belief is saying to yourself "I've got to take the clothes from the washer and put them in the drier". It's not an easy thing when you believe you cannot walk through a door to the laundry room. You believe in your mind of a pain only you can go through. You believe in your heart that it isn't the end of the world. But to clean your clothes seems like the hardest thing in the world. The smell of your stink of your clothes believes in its own way of the pain that accumulated by the soiled clothes.

The clothes represent the world you live in. Clean the outside; yes, but it does not clean the inside. You want to clean the inside, but you don't know how. "Wash thy robes in the blood of the lamb." There ought to be a detergent by that name. Like the chemist in the lab creating new detergents, some mathematics should be made that will cleanse the mind of impure thoughts and ugly rumors and hurtful wishes.

When belief can be washed, then the mind can come clean. The computer keyboard then can be immortalized and honored and worshiped. "Before you clean the speck out of your brother's eyes, take the log out of your own." How can a dirty thing clean a clean thing? The kosher thing is the clean thing. The belief is the thing that decisions thing to get to the rest of the mind. The belief has the angle that shoots to language. Only then does feeling go down to acting, and knowing go to vision. Because feeling can have more than part to it, does belief anchor itself in decision, to even itself out with knowing and vision.

Belief pushes itself to what the rest of the mind has. Belief is that thing you think you know and when challenged decides it thinks it decides. Belief and knowing are like decision and language and vision. To sum it into one word would be feeling. Acting (behaving) is every word wrapped up in itself from beginning to end. Belief is the fuzzy thing that can suddenly become defined into glory. Power and kingdom, too; to Power because of the glory of the self, to Kingdom because of the glory of the Group. Belief is a stabilizer that enjoys its own feedback. Sometimes lonely, in groups, belief is the equalizer giving the group its identity. Presence of clothes shows you are in such a resonant group.

Presence is amplitude of resonance; belief is what divides its own multiplication. Belief adds to its own subtraction. Belief loves decision. Belief is to live for and die for; better to stand for a belief than let it sit by the wayside, fickle and obscene.

Belief—the transistor—can turn itself on and turn itself off. From a transient threshold edge of knowing, belief guides like a subconscious, together in meaning with language, to engage the laws of language, to engage its own '0's and '1's. Belief continues to divide and subdivide, for as long as '0's and '1's are visible.

Belief in the center of a system spews out data. Somewhere like in a donut around the data form of control, belief happens. Belief meets its own belief and knowledge happens. The control knowledge then defines what's outside its own donut. The belief that originated in the first place gets protected and honored and cherished. The knowledge donut has the belief in itself, and also the belief that protects its own belief. Delusions—the false belief—is the belief that protects itself. The donut is in the mind with delusions. The only one who can change the belief is the owner of that belief. Neurotics own the donut; psychotics eat the donut; the psychiatrist makes the donuts.

Belief is the background that mathematics work. To calculate intuitively is a talent that can be built into a skill into a profession. Ideas that are decided and undecided in themselves are felt, seen and spoken in the abstract thing called the mind. The belief in the abstract mind is the concrete will of knowing what is seen.

Belief does not have behavior; belief is the behavior in the unscheduled mind. The schedule said to its own mind's schedule is to plan. But to plan is not always to schedule. A plan coordinates places, while a schedule coordinates places and times. Belief that your date will be at the soda fountain shop at eight o'clock is a schedule, while the plan to enjoy the date is a belief that your plan will work. Plans capture the world; schedules capture the self. Beliefs of self and beliefs of world in a simple mind are the same. The self-aware mind feels both. Belief, the constant spinning that is always coming together.

Books do not contain beliefs. Books are the beliefs themselves. One cannot store a belief except its containment unveils and pokes through its donut fence. Belief combines and makes the greater coordination. A library exudes the belief of belief on the shelves. Like a child, a library is more than one book; each book is a belief; so the library is more than a belief. This wisdom itself a donut. So even is belief met its own belief, to make wisdom. Wisdom only a rider on a horse; the horse of belief not there. The saddle ready to carry wisdom; wisdom, the rider, with stuff to bring to destination, but the horse of experience, determination, and fortitude; behavior, not there. To carry the saddle is its own wisdom when the horse of belief contains its own belief wisdom. The idea of wisdom is its belief, the statement of law, a dream. A distant memory of a very loud thought of childhood. Trusting that love will survive to the establishment of humanity of adulthood. The breaking of trust the beginning of the false belief. But the humility of desperation creates forgetfulness. The future is now; the saddle, with its rider, is on the horse, and the horse now moves in time. The book's beliefs are open; anyone can read. Belief is by and large what we hear. What we hear is accumulated in our ears. The best way to clear our beliefs is to clear our ears. Belief is what we hear. Use medicine to melt the earwax and use warm water to flush out the crud. Belief is what we hear, and what we hear becomes belief, unless it is, melted and flushed.

But if Belief were Dollars—oh yes, that incredible belief that are dollars—we would all be to have lots of ideas—we would all be super powers and super beings like Batman, Spiderman, Superman, X-Men. There would be no food, We would have global communism. The war of ideas would rage rampant. This book would be a contender. If beliefs were dollars, pain would be more real, and the threat of pain, guiltless and without remorse, and every boss a philosopher.

If beliefs were dollars, evil would be rampant, but undisclosed. Kings in different clothes would be paupers. It would be easy to make money, but hard to find goods to spend it on. Wisdom would be the most precious of commodities. The stock market would be overwhelmed by senility and old age. The passing of time would be painful in itself, and new blood would be executed by misers of iniquity. There would be more bags of cash with sixty-five thousand dollars under a bed or in a cupboard hidden.

To clean out a safe would be to say a word. Anger would be the safest emotion. Good sense would be nickels. Carnivals would be dreams. Toxic waste would be parking lots. Anxiety, ticket booths, happening in an elevator. The masks we wear in polite society the jewel's of a king's ransom. A stiff drink would be a stiff drink. A cigarette would be a good way to pass the day. Ignorance would be poverty. Elevators might go to love. The Zero, the greatest Infinity of all. Oh, the Zero it is, known by its own absence. Time writes its own stories, that terror is in patience, and fear, in its kindness. You can never be late for an appointment. Leaving, the greatest happiness.

With belief, trusts are masks, and risks are bathtubs. The greatest mask we put on for others are the ones we take off for no one. But we wash every day for ourselves. Like clothes, what crud is washed away by the belief in power; what crud is washed away by the power of money. The mask of belief that molds to our bodies and forget in our bathtubs. Masks don't always wash out. The larger the bathtub, the larger the belief; the smaller the bathtub, the larger the mask.

There is pain in belief. It hits you in the ears. Deafness is the ultimate hearing that listening that is not hearing. The little bird says, "shrink, shrink, shrink". Hunger betrays you. Like physics, human follow rules even in spite of self's belief.

Belief, The feeling in the book of money. That time absorbs the past of belief of understanding. In the physics of money that we all agree what money is; the library of coins are their own relativity. That belief washes its own containing. With every switch, a superhero emerges. A donut in a bathtub is a system.

Chapter 10

The Nature of Reality

The best reality is the reality adapted to; everyone is in a struggle to know their song, and play it. To press fast forward at sleep at night, and play, again, in the morning. To wonder at the rewind, and fear the stop. Artists record. The best song is the song that listens to itself.

The nature of reality is fuzzy around the edges like the Mandelbrot set. Inside, Mandelbrot is black. Outside, Mandelbrot is white. On its surface, new patterns develop. Life that changes is on the surface of earth that is black in the sky at night yet white in its clouds in both day and night, which is earth's water in the atmosphere. Clouds change with randomness of Mandelbrot.

Order is in randomness that any particular sequence cannot be proven or disproven to be random. How much is random? That which is sequence. On randomness's surface, is to analyze, to translate, and to execute. Nature does these. To analyze in white to execute black, to translate on its surface.

Each moment is frozen and melted in the time sequence under order of fantasy; under randomness of reality; the struggle to be is more important than the struggle to do. The cells multiply by dividing, and the cells divide by multiplication. To know it all is to know it just where you are now—in completeness. More than this you are god.

Sometimes when you feel love—with family—and you find wisdom—and you have your health, and it comes into unity, feeling the whole—then your five fingers feel the list—maybe Thanksgiving of Christmas—you feel as I do the etching onto this page—and I feel the edge like you do—the edge of the open, the edge of the closed—

That before and after of time stuck like a magnet to the present; to write truth, and it is also truly comforting. When it is not calculation yet it is not poetry.

In the darkness you see a light. Do you fix it? Is it fixable? Maybe you should fall asleep and wait for the light to grow. Will it fix itself? Is it easy to be patient or hard to be jealous? How does one be kind to a light in darkness? Is it right to be jealous of the light to want it for yourself?

The dance in one's mind grabs the attention "look at me". Me looks at me looks at me looks at me. The turning of a head to look from right to left and the turning of a body from left to right. "Look at me" do you know if I am learning.

Can I teach it after I learned it. Do I know as a precedence to teach it or is it known at all if it is not communicated. Can one transmit if it is never received. Is it to know a truth a comfort.

Doers stress help to find the light. Does anxiety help to avoid the darkness. Do you love it? Is it loveable? Maybe you should wake up and be kind for the darkness to leave. Will the darkness listen? Will the good finally triumph? The computer stands alone. The computer encodes stress and anxiety and repeats and repeats and repeats. Sometimes it breaks. The light and the darkness is encode in a dance communicated and reflected back into time itself. It looks at it looks at it looks at it. The turning of a zero into a one and the turning of a one into a zero "look at you, look at you".

Do I know if you are teaching. Can you learn it before you learned it. Is it the heart and soul, or is it believed at all, if it is calculated. Can one receive if it is transmitted. Is one engaged at school to learn or does one marry a Job to teach.

Chapter 11

Prelude to Wisdom

Margaret Raymond stepped off the bus that led into town a few miles short. She worked in Des Moines as a registered nurse and social worker and she was on vacation the same way she did every summer. She had opened up her atlas at random and punched a needle on the page with her eyes shut. She went where the needle said. This year, Elksville. Where the fate led her, she was led; Margaret believed in random acts of kindness, and the more random, the better. She woke up so much better when she left the world a little better than the day before.

Elksville was a small town of thirty-five hundred. Major industry, wood and wood products; a minor sawmill stood in the north of the county. There was also a historic site that said Thomas Edison once took vacation there. Being twelve miles away from a major superhighway through the Ozarks, Elksville had the advantages of isolation, yet easy access from anywhere, provided you really wanted to go there.

Margaret Raymond was wanting to go there. Armed with only a knapsack and a cell phone, with money and knowledge of martial arts to comfort her, and her disarming charm and apparent love for ones around her establishing truths to share, she was a true good Samaritan. And Margaret was feeling that Elksville was not prepared for her.

As she followed the power lines on the road into town, walking at an ambling gait, whistling softly to herself, she couldn't help but notice a red—but wasn't green?—barn on the side of the road. It seemed to be going in and out of existence; green fog and transparency, she could see the trees beyond, like there was no barn at all.

She walked towards the apparition. Twisting and turning, Margaret had to use her innate sense that walked mazes so she herself would not disappear herself as she walked towards the barn. "Is this Elksville?" she wondered aloud. First to the left—then to the right—then to the right again—then forward—then . . .

She heard a noise inside and opened the red door . . . it was green, so green, a fog, and time stood still, and time whorled around in eddies and whirlpools . . . it reminded her of so many stories her patients back at the hospital would talk about, how aliens in UFO's had this exact same kind of green fog and time feeling misty and suddenly she felt how special now—now—now was so special—

The green fog lifted, and a Man appeared . . .

Sitting on the floor, looking confused.

- - -

"Why, hello, who are you?" was the first thing Margaret spoke.

His eyes spoke for most of him. He couldn't directly gaze at her, yet somehow he wanted to. "I'm lost"—in a trickle of soft tears—Mannie spoke with a half-way, crazy grin. "I'm lost in a—"

"A maze? A barn? Just tell . . ."

"No, just—wait, don't—leave me alone."

The brown and dark barn hay bin smelled strongly of burnt sugar. Her mind opened in a flash of self-recognition, and Margaret sighed in a way that only committed social workers had. "I suppose you think the aliens don't know you're here?"

"I pray every day, every hour. I've got two bloody altars—one over by that bale of hay"—Mannie pointed—"And another one there by the potter's wheel." Mannie gestured to both places at once with each of his arms. "I'm so rich I don't need electricity. They say that. They say I'm rich. So how come I live in this barn?"

"How come you never go out?"

"They've got oats for the horses over there in that bin—no horse could eat that much in a year. It's tasty for horses—it's tasty for me, I've got water from the hand pump in the trough, and there in the corner, that outhouse. The barn roof keeps the water out; horse blankets for warmth. I'd be a fool to give up this life."

And Mannie cried, mostly to himself, and partly to Margaret, "So now you're here—what are you going to do?"

- - -

The first thing I'm going to do is to bring you into town."

"They don't like me there. I'm an outcast. To them," Mannie, dejected and angry, "I'm a scapegoat. When I first came here—I was strange and crazy to them. All I wanted was someplace I wouldn't be bothered. They ask a lot of questions, you know."

"I can always tell them where exactly you live. This barn. They'll find out eventually, and better to be prepared for that than have them burn all this down."

Three minutes of silence passed. Then resignedly, Mannie, replied, "Okay. I'll go."

- - -

"You can always leave." Margaret said.

"Why would I want to?" Mannie said.

"Don't you see they don't like you?

Why do I have to see? Am I not happy? Don't I not sit here, day to day, week to week?"

"You have to understand," flustered Margaret. 'Just because the human is an animal doesn't mean that the animal is a human—aliens," she explained, "for all their superiority, are not human."

"I mean—well," Margaret continued, "'Superiority' to Elksville is a commodity. Superiority is something bought and sold. You know that. That happens to society that is too big to be just one family, and too small to be a city. And computers buy and sell—you understand computers. I knew your secret when I opened the barn door. You were covering up that electrical cord with straw. That was the smell of burning sugar. The hay shorting the power line. I saw the power lines coming into the barn. Yet you said you were proud to have no electricity. I reasoned—then, after days, yet it came—you were hiding the fact you own a computer. I saw the telephone line on the road, in. Then I knew you must guts, and balls and soul, hooked into the World Computer."

A look of firm indignance covered with anxiety covered Mannie's face. "I'm discovered—private no more—I'm public."

"Yes, all inside your head."

"I had to be isolated" replied Mannie. "Isolated no more."

\- - -

They walked the rest of the way into town as Mannie pointed out particulars of the Ozark nature Margaret never knew. Mannie would point and click with his mouth and a starling with a white patch on its head—which had been following the two for quite a while—would go and snatch an oak leaf and deliver it into Mannie's hand.

Mannie allowed, "in all the world, Man is the most dangerous animal of all." "Especially man's humanity to man", replied Margaret. "So what are you going to do to me?" Mannie came back.

"Remember, Mannie; I'm a woman, not a man." Margaret practically cursed.

\- - -

At the steps of the post office in Elksville the same old crowd sat, in benign judgement of all that passed by them, as they had done last year, the year before that, since time immemorial, at least a hundred years ago. And Mannie courageously walked with Margaret, yet broke into a cold sweat as the large Village Square Clock banged away the time marking mid-afternoon to him, yet exactly three o'clock to the villagers. As Mannie felt the rhythm of the seasons and times, so did the villagers ignore it. Rather just gave reason to scrutinize ever closer in their biased way, biased since time immortal.

\- - -

Paul was at the highest of the post office steps, and recognized Mannie, from a momentary peaceful sideways glance, and suddenly, a scowl of distaste and ugliness came upon his eyebrows, and then the rest of his face.

"We don't like him lady."

A pause happened, in that momentary eternal way, and then Paul added, "If you don't go away, I'll tell the boys here that man's name", gesturing. "Then that'll be trouble."

Margaret stared in her benign, loving way, that melted hard men than Paul, and said nothing, saying everything.

Not too much time passed and Margaret hissed and got out of the way of the psychological bombardment.

"Tell you what—if the farther away this man goes, will you like him better?" Margaret composed herself.

Paul looked around. The fact that he was responsible—only he knew Mannie's name among the group—and he didn't want a lynching, even though it was possible—an he could have—he remembered intuitively that Margaret was a helper, even though a stranger.

- - -

"Tell you what—the Greyhound passes this way in about three hours." Said Paul. "If he gets on the bus, then I won't tell his name, and I'll keep the peace until what time he gets on. If he doesn't get on.—" Paul was hoarse, "then I can't be responsible for him."

The milieu on the steps looked attentive. There were many people they didn't like, and when their names came up, that isolationist hate activated—Yet Paul was their leader, able to read and write, and that paper and letter were the law.

Mannie looked at Margaret. "I'll be on that bus."

They walked quickly back to the barn and Mannie mused resignedly as they walked through the door, and looked around the last time.

- - -

Mannie brushed some straw away from a corner where he slept.

"That's the computer," he pointed.

Margaret did a double take. All it was a keyboard, a regular monitor, and a mouse.

"That's the machine," Mannie grinned, brushing away some straw, grabbed a handle and uncovered a part of the flooring. Wires and circuit boards flowed underneath, uncovering a maze of switching equipment.

"And all this . . . goes to that simple telephone cable up there?" Margaret pointed to the two thing wires going to the ceiling.

"It took me four years to make it look like nobody wanted this place. It was then in Elksville I tried to make friends—but that was years ago—I shouldn't mention it—" Mannie spoke.

- - -

"Look under that door," Mannie said. That's my power source. It's called a Zambini pile."

Margaret saw what looked like a pile of metal sheets atop one another the size of a dishwasher. "How does it work?" she asked.

"You know how a flashlight battery works? That there are different layers of different metals connected by a damp electrolyte?"

"Yes," Margaret said. "So?"

"Each plate of metal there is a full square meter. Basically, it's just a battery that will give off twelve volts energy for over forty-five years without replacement, just sitting there. You could build one in your basement."

Margaret was impressed. "Is this your design?"

"No, actually, it was Thomas Edison who built the first one, like of this size."

- - -

"Look in that box over there," Mannie pointed. "That's the box of money."

Margaret frowned, but stared when she opened it. Disbelief, as she riffled the twenty-dollar bill stacks through her disbelieving fingers. Her instinct was to count it—but she didn't want to rip the bundles apart; they were banded with U.S. Treasury seals stating each bundle was one thousand dollars. There were thirty bundles.

"So you see my need was for total isolation, yet full awareness of what is going on in the world."

"But now you have to get away from isolation."

"No, I have to get away from you."

- - -

A chilly look came over Mannie. "I'll have to leave my machine behind, you know." he said. The spots were in his eyes.

"How did you make your money to do all this here?"

"Do you remember the Norden Bomb Sight from World War Two?"

"Yes."

"Peter Norden was my roommate in college."

"And?"

"He believed in my vision."

After a pause, Mannie continued. "To make the world a better place to live, it needs a god to interact with, . . . some higher form of love. Pete saw it in violence. I didn't, and he was forever in my debt. So I claimed the whole thing—the kindness of the violence towards his neighbor me, became money."

"But . . . so why here? Why so much isolation?"

"It was necessary . . ."

"Oh."

- - -

"We've got to go back to meet the bus." Said Mannie. "I've got to go before they trace my line."

Margaret was still admiring what wasn't in the barn. To live like a human, she surmised, was to live like a beast; to have the friends of animals like birds, rabbits, deer, here was a man who was not a man because he chose a Walden-like setting—yet here he was, with one simple phone line, in touch with the entire world. He had the machine that knew. An agent of global change, alone.

She almost regretted finding him.

They trudged mostly silently side by side back to town.

Mannie and Margaret were talking in obviousness.

"How do I go?"

"You just go to the door of the bus—"

"The Greyhound?"

"Yes—and when the door opens, get in."

"I'll need a ticket?"

"Yes—a ticket to go through the door."

"Then?"

"You sit down in one of the seats.

The driver will start the engine, and the wheels will turn, and the bus will go."

A pause. Then, "I guess that is the way I do go."

- - -

In a little bit, both in the walking and thinking, Mannie announced "I have something to say."

"I'm listening," replied Margaret.

"Suppose there was someone very, very special in the plan of the universe. Say this person was very, very special in the plan of the Earth. Or very important just here, happening to be wandering and just about now."

"Now," he continued, "suppose this person gets on a bus. And call this person an agent, and the system the person—the agent—is on the bus—call it an agent-bus."

Another bit of time passed, and Mannie continued. "Now suppose there is another person as important, as special, as unique, in the plan of the Universe—call this person another agent. And this agent is on the agent-bus too."

Mannie completed his sequence, saying "Now just how important is the agent-bus? For how long is the agent-bus important? How important is the agent-bus's driver? Is the driver more or less important than the agents that are on the agent-bus?"

Margaret thought and replied, "Your point is, I guess, is why the universe is the way it is."

"When I get on that bus, how does the universe change?"

- - -

Chapter 12

Vision

Vision collects itself.
The "AHA!" itself.
Vision is the future going to past. Now is fleeting, but what we have.
Vision is the coordinator.
Vision starts in the eyes and ends in the whole mind.
People are the now of the vision.

Vision's universe starts in the body. The body acts and the mind thinks, vision seems so large, in a world so small.

Vision sleeps and wonders how it sleeps. A growing idea feels its vision and escapes to belief. Belief runs vision as language balances belief and vision. Vision shows the 0's and 1's. Relativity that a common object is seen by two agent-people is relativity's reality.

To agree in relativity runs vision. Vision is the first processor in the mind. Vision starts the decision. Watching vision gets the "AHA!". Watching is a burning of a coldness. Watching is also a freezing of what is hot. Paintings, as art, captures a frame of vision, as poetry captures a frame of language.

To describe is a common. The antenna is the eye-stalk, as the ground is the brain-step. The crystal detector lies in the two eyes and the soul that is in the eyes. Memories are often visual, and words are heard in the ears. Vision is what we see, in perpendicular; ears are at right angles to the voice of what we see.

Writing is a record of what we see; to make noises according to the scratched line of ink from pen to paper: That what is on paper is committed. Vision represents that which is committed among all we see. Paper records our "input" and vision watches the processing and "output" when the capacitance fires its charge in the neurons to freeze its heat. Input is known by the firing of heat into the cold.

Waiting hurts because eyes still vibrate. Eyes still fire neurons connecting truth from false and separation still. "AS" goes in one eye, "TO" the other eye, as the soul "IS".

Choices often hurt decision.
    Because of the cold.
Trust that salve decisions
    Run because of heat.

"Love is a consuming fire"—
    "God is Love"—
        "God is a consuming fire."

"Time is nonexistent—"
    "Time is a triangle—"
        "Time is a nonexistent triangle."

Experience confirms the tracks of the neurons. To go off the beaten track of the neuron is to think; many places are those of thoughts, and thoughts can stay on the same track with ease. It is a big pile of circuits that coordinate vision. What is difficult and what is easy mentally is not always circuited. The track of the neuron firing is as cold and as hot and towards what we would not think mental reality. The crazy man is known by his neuron path. The universe of by easy reality is so.

Vision makes lists all by itself. To be seen is to bounce around and to be heard in its own vibration. Vision doesn't input or output. Vision is a global, gestalt expense of funds the body earns. Vision does not budget but spends heat and earns coolness and death has its wages of sin. Vision is how one learns. Vision is how two learns, and many more, by triggers that the largest frame of dollars are those that dance in the eyes. Vibration the subtle bottom line. Is.

Two people are watching a pile of money. One is worth one hundred thousand dollars and the other is on social security. Say the pile is a thousand dollars in twenties. Which person's view is the correct one?

In the long term—after many visions—there is the big difference of preparation. Both persons look forward to happiness—and how money is a key to happiness, though it is a key itself, and not the happiness itself. If you can get to the store in time, you can have happiness. But who would you feel happiness with more—a warm fuzzy human or a dummy made stuffed with twenty dollar bills?

So vision switches and connects like trains on train tracks. Neurons visible.

Get on, on time; have a destination; trust the conductor knows the switch master on the decisive diverging and converging tracks. Once the path is set, and the switches freeze, to get to the warm and fuzzy destination.

When you de-train, what you rather have—a warm fuzzy body to hold, or dollars spent well that accumulate in your vision? That's a rhetorical question. The fuzzy itself difficult to track.

The train is even a destination by itself. There are those who get warm and fuzzy just for the sake of warm and fuzzy. There are those who sit in coach and watch the world go by. They know they can always get off at the next station and touch the earth itself. Train goes clickety clack, a mesmerizing sound that connects with vision and feeling. There is a feeling that you are both there and now and then. Those twist the trees upside down and make music in the unlimited knowing the emotions of passing greenness. They imagine money was designed and created in the green and white of the passing unknowable sequence of metaphor, simile and prepositional phrases. That the thought of travel finds its specialness in everyday, common things that speed is not for speed itself—but speed is merely to get there.

Such is the vision that the whole world learned when the locomotive and cab and caboose came to be. Soon even the conductor and switchman and engineer became the first "esteemed technicians" to the modern world that locomotion was in the world, but not of the world.

A conductor is not outside the window. A switchman is not inside the train. An engineer is not inside the track and is not outside the train. Nevertheless, the train goes. In those circumstances, no two technicians know exactly the same train. But the train is, nonetheless. The speed was a symptom that passengers enjoyed, to get to their destination in vision.

Vision, that train sequence of thought, is vision, where an impact of Language Law—the resonance is the emotion, that the speed of light is the speed of time. But when the speed goes to zero, the difference is not discernable. Two visions are the same when the speed is high.

And so thus is money is train in vision. Technology is where vision is close to money. The train of thought, there on the train of the track, is the most expensive form of godly money.

Each frame of that vision that in its dissimilar form of action is its own pleasure platform. On that coach trip, vision had is vision made. Sitting still on psychiatric couch, trying to find the big picture, only adds its own metaphor. True healing is not by vision. But vision is how you get from one place to another; not the trip itself. Toss back your eyes, and thread the needle that sits on the phonograph, and you will find religion. You will find the path that the path takes you on. Squeezing the lemon makes the lemonade, if life provides only lemons. Religion best said on the couch is not always the best for life itself. If you have no cups, lemon juice is bitter to the tongue, having no sugar to spice the life.

To fall asleep, start the music. To sleep to engage the language laws even to the extent that feeling is lost. The sleep is yourself getting out of bed. You can't stop the law of sleep; the vinyl record rotates regardless of needle or not. The trickle of electricity generated by the needle is not noticeable without a forceful amplifier. So amplification in Language Law has its limits on its lower side. Strange things happen with large amounts of lemon juice. Do you keep the lemons or try to find a cup? Try to find rational reasons for the thing you do or keep the timing slow—either way, religion will find its vision. Vision, the sleeper.

You can't stop the law of sleep, that vision that vibrates the eyes vibrate the mind into submission, and what ecstacy and terror therein. Rest assured you will dream this. Sleep as a resistance that futility has come hold on. The greater resistance the lesser sleep, that knows thus its own power. The steam itself that heat the electrical water and drives the piston to turn the wheel that runs the locomotive. The vision, thus, that runs the money, and thus, the life.

The famous meet the shore of the sea of life. The famous have vision of their own vision. Ker-Chunk, goes the stamp; La-di-dah, goes the envelope; the letter inside will get to its destination. Shielding communication is a good way of insuring the communication doesn't get lost in its voyage to the learner.

Sketches of battleships and jet planes take place while in class to get a liberal art's degree is what is truly seen by the student. The teacher gently and patiently waits for the student to see in view then say the

"Aha!" to link the things together. Private conversations often lead into vision.

How far can one see when all impediments stop gracefully? Until it hurts. The eye will not let the mind sleep—even hurting. The brain has no pain-sensing cells; the pain being is in the spine. But to see is not always to recognize. Things pop up in awareness like playing solitaire and suddenly you see the red jack can be put on the black queen. Tables of jolly are these. Tunes of babies are the best tunes, tunes of shades of better and worse vision. A baby's soul by looking in the eye creates a connection in a beam, eye to eye as great as a laser cutting steel.

"No, Mr. Bond. I expect you to die!" says Goldfinger. Stocks and bonds, are not as powerful as gold. To look at the eyes of Auric Goldfinger he loves Gold. Its yellow seducing color; its consistency, its weight. As Goldfinger himself has tiny eyes set in a large face on a large frame. He identifies himself in a way that supports his life.

The vision of the movie "Goldfinger" rests on the vice, greed. This is easier to understand than perhaps space-based moonrakers or Dr. No's nuclear island base. Greed is a simple force of vision. On its other side includes love and jealousy.

Who could Goldfinger be jealous of? James Bond. That is why Bond was more valuable alive than dead, that Goldfinger realized in the final moments his industrial laser was to do its work. His jealousy come aware in a way only the silver screen could portray. An egotistic, self-centered vain type of jealousy, but jealousy no less. Goldfinger relates greater greed through love than love by greed. When Oddjob does the number with his hat on the statue, Auric says to Bond, "I own the club." His country club he owns, his place of his love for others who also seek and have gold. The game of possessions; the game of money and worth; Auric's game of Gold, his love.

To love gold was this means of balance in a tiny, shifty pair of eyes "It is a bank . . . closely guarded, perhaps but still, a bank!" to meet his own vision, he builds visual aids for his own edification. And here is where vision is so rich. Auric can sleep with one eye on his greed and one eye on his jealousy, and rest in his sleep of gold. Gold, filling his brain, finally consumed by his own greed to nuke Fort Knox—but its beginning clearly that Auric was jealous man in his youth. Visions can only have so many axes. Visions are meant for minimalism.

The shortest words are the shortest meanings. The vision attaching "I" to anything and the vision attaching "A" to anything.

People have often wondered what is "I". Is "I" the subconscious, the body, the emotions or whatever. I think the "I" invocation tends to move the subject of "I" inside. Like my name "John". I bring myself inside by "I John".

Similarly, invoking "A" brings the subject towards the external. "Family". "A Family". "Love". "A Love".

Vision calls what it takes, and deposits as it gives. Vision are dollars of a man. Control, to a man, is the balance internal contracts from external and internal expands into external. Control—the skin—the containment, the fence, the border—of life, indeed the universe, is made up of vision. Silence is the capacitance in real life. The cup is what holds the cup. What is true at one time doesn't necessarily have vision at that time. Control wants, but does not always have, and sometimes does have.

Vision has no secrets on its own. To be in a place holds secureness; as a fountain flows through its filters and back again. The collection of all neuronic pathways are like sludge through a pebbled stream and some sludge gets stuck on the pebbles. Someone picks out the pebbles and lo and behold, the pebbles are a lustrous yellow, heavy and beautiful. Thus does God meet the vision of the nuggets in the neurons.

A person's reality is in their dreams. One may listen, and not hear, there is a difference between learning and understanding. Vision coordinates understanding that heats to a boil and freezes to a cube. Tears wash out the freon.

Mathematics accepts the coordination of vision. Addition works for everybody. So does division and multiplication and subtraction.

Euclid's axioms seem to work. That's why we remember them. The associative; the commutative; from axioms become postulates through theorems. From assumptions come logic. Systems can be named and limits are inferred. As things work together in the mind, things work together on the Reality Environment. Without logic, the brain falters, even in the study of logic itself. To work on a blackboard, with chalk, the chalk has to touch the blackboard. Without touch, nothing is seen.

Mathematics can know and predict transformations. Vision works even if not understood. Indeed, understanding "understanding" is a mathematic of itself more in love with poetry and computers than mathematics itself. Psychology and electronics play lesser roles. Mathematics, the queen of the sciences, has vision as her mate.

Understanding is not wisdom, but understanding "understanding" is. Repetition makes neuron tracks that enlarge the neuron nuggets in the electrical water that absorb pain and points toward pleasure—but it is not pleasure itself. A vision of pleasure is often pleasure itself.

The mind is as big as it thinks it is. The mind looks at itself; the mind has a vision of itself; and out comes a pulse, and the mind feels the pulse, and some kind of hill is conquered, then the mind forgets in some conquest of another hill—until there is no more hill, and there is only pulse. The mind engine that refuses to work is a contradiction and a mental illness. The mind works even as pleasure and pain are felt, regardless of vision. Vision here is not vision there. Vision is still coordination.

Is there a control in vision? Yes. It is called eyelids. When eyelids are shut sleep happens. Sleep is the mind looking at itself because eyelids are shut. Blinking at an amazing thing when one doesn't believe their eyes. Reality is heightened in eyes closed. One kisses with eyes closed? Yes. What controls eyelids? I know right now you are blinking your eyes right now. Eyelids are politics, and politics make strange bedfellows. In one bed are two sets of eyelids. Don't fall asleep at the wheels of an automobile. Eyes need to be open to sense the moving landscape.

Eyes are the mirrors of the soul, and eyelids are the dollars of the soul. Rest in peace, of the dead whose coins rest on eyelids, removed at burial to bring good luck to the coin's owner. How eyelids can be so powerful, close to death and close to life. A dream that enables one to die in ones sleep is surely coordinated with the eyelids.

The attitude of eyelids surely drive the direction of vision—in to out. Deja Vu—the sense of having been somewhere before actually being there—is an eyelid confuser. To sleep with eyes open is also difficult.

Vision does not usually see its own word. Vision is in the back of the head. Vision is its own sensor. Vision has the ego under its control. Vision does the imbalance back into its own structure. Vision has its fear of going beyond what it can see. Vision is narrower than it is wide. Vision resonating at evil as it has amplitude by time is good.

Prophecy makes its true manifestation in vision. The facts of a thing's manifestation diverts to vision. But what does a body do with vision that might be artificial, so what is real? Vision maintains reality, but is not real itself, not only unfelt, but unbelief, not knowing, and assumes its own will, in a dangerous force of its own denying existence. It is vision's usefulness that keeps vision as a pillar.

There are many clicks that compose a clock. The escapement that makes modern clocks possible—its own clicks—is the true function of vision that keeps society's timing regular and together. Seeing, a regular thing, has feeling inside vision. Clicks are subjects of a vision that loves its body. It is the body that freezes itself to not absorb itself in the outside of its container. Vision helps to establish edges of containment. Vision's reality is felt in containment. To use reality is to enable vision.

Vision does not want itself. Vision wants its own containment. Vision wants security. Vision wants to know family. Vision is thus a feeling of a female thing. Vision has the "0" with a circle that rotates in its own circle of pleasure. "Oohhh . . ." The endless cycles of an ending feeding back into a beginning that ecstacy turns into a meaning of light. The disagreement finds a token of assent and the argument folds into a new thread. Communication's Psychology is in the female. The edge of awareness that is called consciousness is necessarily "0". If the edge of awareness was "1", containment would contain itself. So "1"'s must be briefly with "0".

Vision keeps discerning that there must be "0"'s and "1"'s that if there weren't—goals would not be goals themselves. It is the goal that vision keeps alive. The vital imbalance that makes a body learn is love inside vision.

Love inside vision is its own vision. If it were not, "1"'s would push each other, and "0"'s would make no sense. But there is love inside vision. It is not easy to understand love inside vision. It upsets its own vision. But eyelids still can close and open themselves, wanting its own love.

Chapter 13

The Main Idea

I just wanted to write down a couple of ideas I have about the future of what computing may bring to the world. None of these ideas are simple in execution, although in principle may bring a lot of love and peace and concert and happiness to the world, if constructed. Whether or not intelligent life exists outside this earth surely is tied to the ideas I am presenting. If these ideas are real, then intelligent life outside this planet surely is closely tied to this technology, for the ideas I am presenting are surely global and universal in their construction.

The first idea is that the internet as now in place has several stages of development to go through. It is nowhere near done now, in the year 2000. The computer should be as simple as a coke machine—to deposit quarters, press a button, and you get your drink to slake your thirst. What is explained here is how you, an average user, would use my vision of the internet.

Your choice, which should only be once a month, would first "get its quarter"—you would either state to your computer what goods or service you as a human could afford. For example, if you worked in the garment district, you could state how many shirts size medium long sleeved you have. Or, if you were a truck driver, you could state you are a truck driver, with a refrigerated compartment of a thousand cubit feet. Or, you could be an owner of a gasoline filling station.

A particular computer—in the internet—would have its own birthminute. The birthminute should coincide with circumstances particular to that computer's software existence. For example, social security computers should birthminute towards the beginning of the month—day 1 minute 0 through day 7 minute 1439. (24*60-1).

At the trigger of the birthday of example computer "xyz", xyz collects presents of computer data and programs peculiar to what that computer exists. For example, a farm computer would get weather forecasts on its birthminute. A garment computer would get the new french fall fashions. Lumberjack computer would get new addresses of rope manufacturers.

My computer has a lot of poetry inside it. When I sign on for my monthly time, all I have to do is to type what I have for the network. There must be an infinite negative balance for me, and for everyone. The Lord's Prayer: "Forgive us our debts as we forgive our debtors". The Golden Rule: "Give unto others as you would have to yourself." The credit of the Earth must be within the credit of One Person.

There would be no financial credit/debit in my scenario, no buying or selling. The computer network would be designed to LOVE—to redistribute goods; to feed the hungry, to clothe the naked, to visit the imprisoned, to cure the sick, shelter the homeless. The computer could do what Reaganomics policy intended humans to do; to reduce taxes, keep government spending. Trickle-down economics if embodied in machines could trickle-down: trickle across, trickle by, trickle for, trickle of.

I also believe that we, as a planet, are not the only planet with life in the universe; intelligent life surely exists out there—but also us. There should be an "Alien Waiting Base" somewhere, probably on a February 29 Birthminute. The military-industrial power base will benefit from Alien landing; the government who gets the biggest chummy—comradeship from Aliens will naturally be the Biggest Government on earth. But probably at the same time, the biggest food service company in the world will probably get the Alien Lunch Franchise—the coveted "ALF" award . . .

"News", as we know it, in newspapers and tv and books and magazines, would still go on as we know it—the only difference is that social issues would be intelligently debated, with the good of community more highly appreciated, and natural disasters given more space than an expose of cruel tv personalities. Legalities would distribute themselves over the Net. The biggest politician would be the biggest programmer. To lead you have to serve; today's oil-run politicians society of kickbacks and bribery works, but just not very well.

Chapter 14

Wisdom Post-Partum

Jeff looked up at the sky and thought that wouldn't it be nice if clouds had different colors. More than white, and more than grey, and more than drizzly black, that would be nice.

And Jeff got up to eat supper with his mom, Margaret Raymond. They had stew, which was delicious. And Jeff went to bed, after first saying his prayers, and Jeff was happy how the Lord had blessed him and his mom and how the thoughts just tumbled out of his head into his mouth, and how the earth seemed to be happy with him, and how the earth had been good to him. He knew he thought differently than other people his age (Jeff was in the first grade) and he thought he might grow out of it. He asked himself every night, "When shall I grow old, away from the earth so my clouds in my eyes will turn different colors and go spinning out into the earth's sky and the sky will be earth no more?"

Suffice it to say that Jeff really didn't think this way. He saw the world in different ways than others; Alan was smart and he knew this. He wanted to be caught away from the humdrum life lived out by his parents and his schoolmates, and even the games played out by his classmates and the games he saw on TV really didn't challenge him. Transformers and Thundercats were not for him. He needed something better.

And Jeff prayed and slept.

It was around the sixth grade that Jeff found his first love: computers. He found an escape, a perfectly real form of existence where things were alive, dancing and fluttering on the TV screen, and fingers could bounce against a keyboard to actually <u>do</u> things with his universe. He found utter contentment in programming, and he vowed it would be his life's work.

Then when he went to bed and prayed, and occasionally remembered his mother's stew and the clouds, he would relax and let his mind relax to better days. And here he was, only in the sixth grade.

Jeff imagined as a sixth grader would. He imagined the universe was a computer, with an operating budget in the trillion trillion trillion dollar range. Jeff imagined he knew the computer that ran the universe; he had several pennies, which he thought was a giant amount.

But Jeff was proved wrong by his own universe, when his pennies were merely that: pennies. The universe that had kept him warm happy and comfortable was in reality his mother and his father had something to do with it. And one day while climbing a tree, he fell, and the universe that had loved him through his pennies was unhappily comforting that his future of the mind was clear, his body would have some catching up. The emotions ran always then, as he woke up to the lights of new days, how his own imagination would catch itself running away with some new patterns of the pennies. The pennies bought chess pieces; the pennies bought old presidents to life, but had no stitches in time for to know how to meet the giants of presidents of those days. Dollars were as far away as what he remembered them to be, years ago, when he would see his father's paychecks from the government go from in the mail to somewhere called a bank, where money was supposed to go to and then disburse to get electricity, heat, food, and blankets. He could not imagine imprecision in these banks; they were steady, and calm, and ubiquitous in their managing of families, of which he was in. That was the source of his pennies. They originated from "The Father". And somehow in his crippled state, after the fall, when the love in his family had a humanistic feel to it; his naming of what was all around him changed subtly; and so the money that he had and was, shifted to a different frequency, and could not absorb the life and light that was so necessary for existence—that came from the pennies.

Jeff worked on his homework as a matter of course. Before he knew it, he was understanding things he didn't know he could comprehend. His life was full of wisdom. Waiting for God patiently, and abiding in His love, he thought time would pass quickly, and to engage the sum of all knowledge and the exchange of information as a translator, was the simple truth of the computer. He thought words exchanged themselves at a cellular level; that chromosomes within cells were data patterns that did exactly what was programmed into them—that mistakes in the cosmos were unthinkable. But when Jeff was in the computer room of his school all he could think of were other computer students—his accident raged on like he wasn't living in his own time—that the computers actually were the link to his other existence. Bugs were things that weren't supposed to happen; what the nature of an error was a necessary opportunity for God to reveal his handiwork, and make love to humans and the humans around.

And one day while the computations were buzzing simply around his head, and as Jeff was in the 23rd century, Jeff had the idea that he should bring the computer from that century into his own time. His pennies allowed it; the cost to bring it through time was not that expensive. There was a Russian language class he was in; the permanence of the work made it clear that the 23rd century central computer could do it.

But suddenly, as rapidly as he thought it up, the computer in his mind left. Jeff figured it was that he was obnoxious and unkind to the cosmic computer. Jeff invited the Computer to supper; a robot came in its place. There was no room for love; yet love was the all-consuming passion, and the neighborhood kids assumed all of time was located in the robot. It was a weird-looking chess partner that you would assume it to be a geek, just by looking. The terrible haircut; the taped on nose thick horn rimmed glasses; the beak of a nose where a simple dimple would had sufficed.

But Jeff endured the other kid's taunting, but he knew that there were mathematics he could not state, but were purely imaginary, and could not stay real for very long. The square root of negative one, for instance. The robot had to look Jeff straight in the eye, and had to tell him a story. But Jeff didn't know the meaning of a flashing light.

And time went on, and on, and on.

- - -

It was Graduation.

There was a tear in Jeff's eyes as he rolled up to receive the Special Award; the computer was running in his wheelchair. The change was happening. Asking nobody for help, his sitting figure was a black form in his modified robes; his wheels were turning under perfect control, rotating up to the podium, knowing the reality of disability. Jeff was basking under the red lights of graduation's attentions. The lights of where the mental dance is; the location of the universe of perfect poetry; deciding poetry's begging in the sunrise of the time of knowledge. The change and transformation heralded first by the passing of the Test; secondly, by the money, by the love, by his family, there in the audience. Mostly, though, it was in Jeff's eyes.

The shortness of breath was deafening his own ears; something it had never done before. The Pride in the entire courtyard, and loudest there in the front row by the other graduates, had a timing that everyone knew of, but never could pin down, the source of that perfection's time. But somehow in Jeff the crowd could see what timing was by the absence of regularity. The wheelchair Jeff rode in made a subtle change in the planned ecstacy of graduation that everyone could notice. The crowd never understood the poetry, but they loved the reciting of it, unanimously.

The crowd came to achieve the weather and the hail of the kudos and the love to Jeff. Jeff's eyes, misty with great and wonderful chemicals leaving his brain through the tear ducts, were waiting for the time to reveal the truths, which was why he was being given the Reward of the Passing of the Test. The crowd agreed he knew. That was why he knew. The table of food plentiful was being prepared behind the crowd, in the field, and the celebration was soon to begin.

The time slithered and groped its way like a snake and woke a primal passion of the accomplishment of his code. The code he wrote to prepare for the Test. It was the spirit of Great and Terrible. It was the machine Jeff controlled—the essential mainframe; the pernicious mini, the arrogant pc; the decisive networks and the emotional servers and the visual printers. Jeff controlled the keyboard that awaited the touch of the finger to the key—the polarities of the ones and zeroes—the sensitive code the cpu commanded. The Code Jeff Wrote; the Word in the Love, and eternal Love the receiving the love was achieving—its rhyme, its integrals, its derivatives. It was the Day of the Lord.

With a rush of feeling the neurons fired and fired back. The neurons of Jeff were firing and made the wonder and the glory. That the roar of the crowd was simultaneous with his own mind; they mirrored and amplified like a laser beaming and burning a path to ecstacy. The crackling of the inner fire was a god that was love. It reminded Jeff of a Do-While loop. Or the Beatles on-fire, "We all live in a nested subroutine . . ." A subroutine beginning with Birth and ending with Death, with permutations and combinations and code of the universe coordinated by a mysterious force known as God.

Jeff had begun in the kindergarten of life. He moved onto the grade school of love, cooperation, and fair play. He became a risk-taker in the middle school of trust. He achieved in the high school of wisdom. Now, in the college of creation, the school Jeff now was graduating from, he knows that he can indeed, accomplish . . . but for how long will it last.

- - -

George, on the podium, the headmaster of the college, is droning on and on as headmasters have their privilege every graduation. "All you graduates before me, having satisfactorily completed the syllabus of studies that make you now, the graduating class of 2000, the focus and the driving motivation of all life on earth—we look to you, as you choose your placement in society, to make, improve, preserve our planet. The technology is before you. I invite all, to implement the changes necessary; the year 2000—the anniversary of the birth of Christ, the philosopher of Pain and Love . . ." George droned on.

- - -

Jeff's mother, Margaret, was in the audience listening attentively. The pain of all her yesterdays were dissolving in the triumph of the moment. The years of the disability and the drive to succeed and the catastrophes of failure and the enduring of stress and the moments of despair and the nights of faith and the decisions for hope and the daily struggle to survive seemed a blank in his mind as the life-moment—promised for every man—was fulfilled in the desire in the audience to appreciate, and planned for by George, to know and to recognize what the students achieved. The discipline of pain was finally transcended by that moment called Love.

- - -

"All This", dreamed Jeff, "Is good."

"I know what is happening. It is love. It is kindness. I've waited and worked for this moment. I know what I must do. Whatever this wheelchair, I'm going to do it. I don't know how long it will take me. Even if I have to wheel across the country. If I have to endure. I have to write the poetry of the computer like this what I'm feeling now. The philosophy of what it is to endure. My special award demands it."

Jeff got to the Podium and George extended his hand and they shook. The Computer, the whole crowd thought, has its New Beginning Here and Now . . . Margaret proud, admitting her vanity to herself.

Jeff thought, as did his mother Margaret, and headmaster George seemingly all at the same time, "His poetry must be the lights of where the mental dance is; the location of the universe of perfect poetry; poetry's begging in the sunrise of the time of knowledge." They all felt a shortness of breath. The race for a philosophy of computing had begun.

But somehow, Jeff felt, it had already been written.

Chapter 15

"Poetron" Theory

A Poetron is a unit of physical existence.

Understanding in space—three dimensions of—in time—in rhythm, music, sequence, harmony, ideas, systems, cosms, almost up to existence itself.

The Poetron is the physical manifestation of thought.

Thought in sequence creates poetrons.

#1. A Poetron is a physical unit of a point that explains and/or describes itself.

#2. A Poetron has an equidistant set of points with a range of zero, which is itself.

Poetrons function under the electric laws of reverse inductance; that close sympathetic vibration will eventually repel other poetrons.

The Poetron is actualization of the Minsky Agent theory, with a broader spectrum to encompass cells and cell containment.

In Minksy's "Society of Mind", part 29.8, labeled "Metaphors", is a poetron almost assembled that says that 'the brain' is 'the eternal 'is'.

That scientists like Volta and Ampere used the metaphor of electricity as pressures and flows of fluid—that Minsky is able to describe that a metaphor is "that which allows us to replace one kind of thought with another".

In every poetron, lies this latent ability to replace itself with something else, and somehow keeping the same kind of thing in the mind as that ability goes.

Then, because we in the inspection of what the mind is, we come across the word 'metaphor', and get blocked in the next thoughts. To realize the Poetron is to 'reset' all those commands that are in the thought buffers in our minds that were blocked—and get to a different level of 'the eternal is' that is.

"In the society of mind" is where Minsky dwells. It is a good bet that there is a specific sequence of activity well hidden in obvious agencies for he to reset his daily commands. As a society of small agents, where the microcosm has no identity, and the macrocosm deals with immediate changes on potential scales, the 'wholeness' in Minsky poetrons are most certainly physical manifestations.

So in there, poetronics is (are) way(s) to predict the future. When a handle can get onto a thought, that thought can be poured into a different thought, and yet retain that thought's concept in every agent in every society of mind.

The easiest poetron is, a poem. A poem is a thought in sequence; it has physical existence; it need not engage in larger or smaller poetrons. It need not make sense, or convey emotion, or to describe any physical condition. A poem, it has been said, is measured by its 'success'—whether or not it does, what it sets out to do. It can be said everything starts out as a poem, and everything stretches to meet it.

So, to call the word "Poetronics", is to call those poetrons that stretch to computation—that stretch to control—to stretch to power. To call something a poetron is to set it up to explain itself, and to recognize its zero radius of equidistant points.

The poetron does not need to associate itself anywhere. Unfortunately, human beings need some kind of grounding to associate any idea—and thus any poetron—with another inside the human mind.

Free association, a technique of psychology, doesn't essentially become a poetron. What free association does become is a system of thought. Psychological healing is the sequence of thought engaged with the subject's emotions to cope with the human's environment. It could be said that everything and everywhere is a poetron, but this is self defeating that the poetron "exists without existing", and leads to the human mind, nowhere.

The Hegelian idea of "synthesis is thesis and antithesis" can screw the human mind up further. The idea of an 'antipoetron' gives the emotion of want. There cannot be—unless psychosis doesn't accept poetrons anyway—an emotion of want of nothing. There can be bliss; there can be greed; but satisfaction of want of nothing creates poems that simply don't make sense. It hurts when a thesis becomes its own synthesis—it hurts when a synthesis becomes antithesis—because the poetron is being wrenched away from itself.

In neurobiology, it makes sense that biological representations of information and memory and processing use some poetronic representations. DNA strands that contain huge amounts of data in extremely small space must most likely use poetrons in intermediary steps to a whole organism like a rat, an elephant, or a human. That the physical representation of poetrons become their own structure in building towards other structure. It could be that if the universe is indeed made of physical quanta in a godlike matrix, the poetron is easily the 'voice in the wilderness' that proclaims light, yet is not light, itself.

To achieve calculation, communication, and power with the poetron, it makes sense to write poetry about the poetron. With calculative power that describes computation; with communication power that are words, and power that influence behavior in both the communication, calculation, and power of behavior itself. That's a mouthful, but it starts from the mouth, anyway.

I hope to make it clear the difference between the 'poetron' and the system 'poetronics'. The 'poetron' signifies the individual thought's reality as what it is itself. "Poetronics" are the laws—the limits, the structures, of what poetrons assert themselves to be. What poetrons you may have at the beginning of the day may change slightly by the end of the day—poetrons floating around, dreamlike, or concrete, like getting a tooth pulled at the dentist,—that exist whether or not the poetronics say themselves to be. Getting beyond awareness of three space dimensions and a time dimension—the introduction of musical, organized, beautiful truth that poetrons provide behind the scenes, and on the stage—get organized, the reality quantized to the beauty/truth level.

For example, a male poetron and a female poetron can get together—and with reverse inductance, they push themselves away from each other. But what happens before that inductance, and what happens after that inductance, is a free—for—all, with witness poetrons, and teaching poetrons, and structures we all have as a humanity collective, the unity of love is easily felt. But with conditions, clauses, and fixed process control in that cosmos, lack of feeling too easily leads to bad decisions.

Chapter 16

Consumer Health Measurement

Part Zero

Once I attended a conference/workshop in an afternoon
with Dr. Grant Mitchell and about a hundred consumers about
methods of consumers of mental health services to improve to a
'person centered' environment. It was great in concept but yet
required a way to monitor all the traffic of the services taking place.
Nothing much came out of that conference except my desire to
express in computer terms the needed software design. So here
I am many months later with this model of mental health consuming
measurement.

Part One

Needed: a Computer Program
To be used by government
    to
"Predictor" of consumer behavior
"Monitor" of consumer activity
"Tracker" of consumer history

Part Two

Executive part of the Computer Program is
Command—control continuum

That manages in a person-based, dream-fulfilling package to transfer
between
Consumer w/relative base
Service provider base
Advocacy base

In a binary, "yes or no" significant condition
of the emotional state of the consumer
    keeping track over time
in the "spread" of service providers
    both existing, being built, and dreampt

Part Three

The Consumer Base of the Computer Program is
The locked portion of the program
Whose nouns include name, address, and time
    The name of the person of its block
    The address of the person (can be reached)
    The time of enrollment in the Program

Whose verbs include load, save, run
    To load the Program with old and new information
    To save the working parts of the Program for its block
    To run the clearing of nonworking parts of block

Part Four

Dealing with the person-situation of the Environment

The consumer data—the typed history of the consumer

The consumer want—the typed description of what is wanted

The consumer sequence—typed what consequences happened
           as a result of initial data and initial want

To such levels that pre-program and post-program the consumer
is satisfied.

Person-situation can also be called the "cosm" of an individual.

Part Five

Discrimination among equivalents

> All objects have names
>> An object is a data-want sequence
> All labels have data
>> A label is a type of object
> All values have worth
>> A value is a discrete want

Part Six

load data—"Dimension"
"Load the program" with data of consumer
  Nervous? Yes or No . . .
  Denying? Yes or no . . .
  Wisdom? Yes or No . . .
  Memory? Yes or No . . .
  God? Yes or No . . .
  Blood? Yes or No . . .
  Command? Yes or No . . .
  Sex/love? Yes or No . . .
  Length/patience? Yes or No . . .
  Water? Yes or No . . .
  Reputation? Yes or No . . .
  Cash? Yes or No . . .
  Spirit? Yes or No . . .
    Other "yes or no" to quantize consumer states
    At initial consultation, and previous times.
Or if Program executes with Fuzzy Logic, these
yes/noes could convert to "0 to 1 reals".

"Lock" of time—of initial consultation,
  And obligation of all parties.

Part Seven

load want—"Address"
"load the program" with consumer want
This is the administration/government part that
Monitors each part and in/of the whole to insure
The Program works.

Part Eight

load sequence—"Externalization"

the emotional commitment of consumer/with relatives
to the Program

Part Nine

save data—"Manipulation"

what service providers contain already, give up to
the Program.

contains namelock and timelock—
immutable name and time of use of consumer

Part Ten

save want—"type"

Advocates prepare for installation into Program what
Tracker needs. What did the Program decide/recommend
for the consumer, report by Advocacy.

Part Eleven

save sequence—"input"

matching lists of possible service activities to list
from Program via Advocates of consumer sequences.

Adding new service providers goes to a master list,
with 'keyword' matching

Part Twelve

run data—"Internalization"
Commit current information to mass storage,
and retrieves into current document from mass storage.

Part Thirteen

run want—"statement"

predict futures of consumer based on current knowledge.
This is the Predictor module that 'completes the sequence"
of the consumer. Results are privileged towards consumer.

Part Fourteen

run sequence—"output"
    Prepare report of current consumer activities,
        In terms of Predictor, Monitor, and Tracker
    In/of/by data and functions of Program

Important "binary" results in Output—
psychosis? Yes or no . . .
unity? Yes or no . . .
Constant? Yes or no . . .
environment? Yes or no . . .
Water? Yes or no . . .
Queue? Yes or no . . .
Reputation? Yes or no . . .
Sex-truth? Yes or no . . .
Depth? Yes or no . . .

There is a Lock of Place now.

Chapter 17

Bajak Interrupt Theory

Ownership of a theory of the universe is how a universe occurs. That existence, in the cognitive sense, understood—is both a physical and mental model of a universe. That physics depends upon cognitive science for its interpretation, and perhaps on the physics themselves in a relative sense.

Borrowed from the computer sciences, the nature of interrupts in a physical computer microchip shows a nature of a universe. Interrupts in a microchip have three different characteristics. The type of interrupt has a characteristic involving different number of variables. How many variables an interrupt contains determines part of the identity of that interrupt type.

In any computer system N is the simple; is the complex; and is the vectored, types of interrupt. The simple is the "Do Interrupt", that is, "Do X". The simple has one variable; that which of where to go; that which of what to do. An actual example is the command in the older 6800 microprocessor microcode instruction in which the value contained in the word of memory immediately following an instruction code is an actual memory address within the first 256 words of memory (in hexadecimal, (0000-00FF)) which contains the operand of the instruction. Such type of interrupt saves cycles of execution versus complex or indexed.

The complex interrupt is "Do X at Y". That is, look at variable Y to do X. In a human being two variables influence each other, and is a dichotomy unresolved when X cannot balance with Y. Yet it is not always that objective in a mechanized world. The world of Pavlovian classical conditioning vouches for such a complex dependent, independent world. Such a type of interrupt is most common to the world at large.

The vectored interrupt is perhaps most spiritual of the three. "At X, do Y to get to Z". That is, knowing where X is—a value of X connected that what X is—does Y as a process—to arrive at Z; new value of the process. The universe constantly in biologic and chemical and physical states do this. A green leaf on a tree X has a process Y photosynthesis and becomes brown in fall Z. The earth revolves around a sun X with process Y of gravitation to new value Z to new position of earth. Mathematics itself depends on the vectored interrupt to tend to balance its own equations. Or sodium and chlorine combine to make salt.

So in summary we have:

Simple—"do interrupt"
Complex—gives address of interrupt to do
Vectored—gives data of address of to do interrupt

So now, to have a complete theory of everything, all we have to do is to assume a reality of computational survivability. All we have to do is to have something to make sure of aliveness. All that has to be is a system that can be perceived. All there has to be are "X, Y, and Z". In mathematics; then there is a reality of equations balancing. In computing, then there is the reality of program functioning. In poetry, the survival of the poet; in electronics, the reduction to practice; in psychology, the organism's survivability. In any area, theme, group, set or containment that has computational survivability has this Bajak Interrupt Theory. But that which is dead; cannot compute; equations unbalanced; no poetry; nothing working; does not have interrupts in the system, and therefore, is unexplainable.

But there is an interesting consequence of this theory: time travel is allowed. Actual "reality bending" can go on; as long as the experiencer survives. As long as something has the interrupts to it, it will be. The question will become, "What is the test of that reality?" So the new question becomes, "Can a system understand reality?" because the notion of reality implies directly the theory of interrupts. Ths means that "The tree falls in the forest and it does not make a noise." A system can survive and yet not be reality consistent. Witness schizophrenia and psychosis. Part of a human's life can be totally inconsistent with other areas yet survive as physical being.

A system need not even be self-consistent. If it functions under interrupt-driven reality, no matter how complex the interrupt, if it fulfills that—anything else can be added or subtracted from that system. That there must be (X,Y,Z) is not even not allowable. That there must be an establishment of the idea of a containment that interrupts are a requirement and logical extension of and an interrupt of itself in our "experience matrix" we call the memory of our brains and the memory and control in our computers and the observed existence of earth and universe. Some invisible triangle pictured in our minds or a triad somewhere in a furthest galaxy is all that is necessary to exist . . . because interrupt theory says we can come from it, or go to it, or know where we are to get there.

Chapter 18

The Brain/Computer Possession

Thought First, was "I am halfway through being ninety years old." I was forty five years old, plus six months. About halfway through 2008. I felt myself rotating one hundred eighty degrees, and pushed the button on the retrorockets.

A little while later, I realized "there is more time in death than there is time in life." This is a fundamental bit of wisdom, that realizing it, creates deeper and deeper axioms of philosophy—not just wise in itself, but wise in process, structure, and limits.

Then coming to now, I saw the brain as a computer—that the brain is a computer. I saw how. The primary function of the brain is to possess. Possession. Ninety percent or so. I want to leave ten percent free.

In mental illness: "The fear of being possessed". To lose one's mind the most awful of destinies. The inner engineer that maintains mental health, exposed; if the inner engineer dies, the body becomes worse than dead.

Or spirits possessing the mind. The mind's body being interrupted towards tasks that it knows can never be accomplished. The psychosis of a wrong possession. The neurosis of a lost possession. The depression of, and the manic with, bad possessions you can't get rid of.

Or the health of mental illness: Give the person a sense of possession. Belonging in a group; give substance that the person can possess.

Or the staff and nurses and doctors in a mental hospital—to give by taking away. That the staff feel superior because of what the staff possesses. That the staff can take away possessions. But for the recovered, their soul can never be taken away. And the acute, or the forensic, the cycle continues, possessions come and gone. Especially the realization that possession never really changes.

The want, and the control, lies in the bridges and fences, of possession. So obvious. Exchanging goods and services for money. Money that buys rent and food. Containment of a body is most certainly not containment of possession itself.

So blindingly obvious that it occurs in every waking day; in every list we make, in every program we participate in; every routine, in substance or etherial; the desire to understand has the impetus to possess.

"Oh, I understand that!"

A Paycheck—how much is it? Is it fair? Is it too small? And you hold it in your hand, the check, and possess it. In a bank account, hidden behind routing numbers, a dollar amount of how much you possess—not essentially what you are worth. You go to deposit it. The possessions accumulate.

A magazine subscription, and you get an issue this month. What's in it? Anything interesting? You possess the magazine, and you read it; to look for possessions in the classifieds column; any baubles or trinkets in the advertisements?

A club membership renewal form in the mail. Is this club worth it? To pay the dues to get the advantages of being in the club. Possess a club, or possess the membership in the club?

What do you value—what do you spend? Are the two related? Possessed of debt, or possessed with responsibility? In the real, real world.

So in possession of nine-tenths of my own life, the bottom line of my own real, real world is that I don't have to possess to be happy. But it does help.

This wish to hurt one's self—to commit suicide—to slash wrists—is to relieve one's self from possession of its self.

"To Love One's Self" is in pain to relieve mental pain by releasing itself to not-self. In Mental Illness, nine-tenths of it is over possession. "Patience is a virtue" in human relations. To Me? To Others? Is protection—Security— having a fence—around My spirit.—to know True Function—to gain by giving away? To worship the hand that feeds you?

To say to one's father, "I don't care whether you say yes or say no—Just make up your mind! And stick to it! Will you give me a big meal tomorrow? Will I sleep on your time?"

The only sure thing is absence—a decision in itself. To share non-awareness changes minds—especially mine. To the Father, and to my earthly father, I become absence myself, by your absence.

That I am your possession simply disappears. Free Will, even though we both agree there is none, by your absence, we contradict ourselves, and contradict, each other. Maybe Now, we commute our relation to stable.

Even in your non-being, father, (physically dead) you could bring me a dream I can possess, because that is my primary function.

Chapter 19

"The Society Bajak Map"

"Without being in the mind", real . . .
Most usually relegated to unconsciousness

Personalities

"What is a brick?" Is anything as solid? Metaphorical control . . .

ICE	I'nternal	C'ontrol	E'xternal				
	Data	Want	Sequence	Statements			
				Commands	Load	Save	Run
				I	C	E	

$$I + C = E \qquad \text{"Total system freeze"}$$

$$C = E - I \qquad \text{"Light shed"}$$

$$I = E - C \qquad \text{"Sense of self"}$$

$$\frac{I}{E} = C \qquad \text{"Ring world"}$$

Movement can happen

$$\frac{I}{C} = E$$

"Inter-dimensional"
Data can happen

$$E * C = I$$

"Complexity"
Communication can happen

Where 'begin' and 'end' are undefined with no real meaning

When word "end" Cause/Implied "Data new"

When word "begin" Cause/Implied "Data real"
assuming intelligence machine, temporal, human, divine, whatever. "Intelligence"

The Moving Ring—
  Architecture allowing dissimilar worlds to match in virtual construction.

World Theory—
  Constructing worlds to match moving-ring construct.

Internal / Control / External

  Internal / Control / External virtual constructs ARE ICE with complexity.

-        -   -

"The Tendency towards C is Universal"
                              "Light seeking"

Words with ICE properties:

	I	C	E
Until	No	No	Yes
With	Yes	Yes	Yes
For	Yes	No	Yes
By	Yes	Yes	No
To	Yes	No	No
Against	No	Yes	Yes
While	No	Yes	No

-     -   -   -

"Where I rules", General Tendencies

"A"	To	External
"I"	To	Internal
"the"	To	Control
"of"	To	multiply
"by"	To	divide

-     -   -   -

Tendency towards I'nternal

| More | I: | Memory |
| | | Plus   Minus   None   All |

| More | E: | Calculation |
| | | And   Not   Or   Not-and |

Tendency towards E'xternal

| More | I: | Input |
| | | Spirit   Truth   Comfort |

| More | E: | Output |
| | | Father   Son   Spirit |

Resting in C'ontrol

More	I:	Address	Place
Resting	C:	Type	Person
More	E:	Statement	Time

-     -   -   -

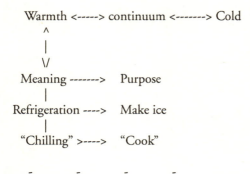

```
Warmth <-----> continuum <-------> Cold
        ^
        |
        \/
    Meaning ------->    Purpose
        |
  Refrigeration ---->   Make ice
        |
   "Chilling" >---->   "Cook"
```

-        -   -   -

Wisdom — understanding the father
discernment — understanding the map
judgement — understanding the purpose

-        -   -

Decision = wisdom discernment judgement
vision = wisdom discernment
language = wisdom judgement
feeling = wisdom
belief = discernment
judgement knowing = discernment
acting = judgement

-        -   -

mind = {decision, vision, language}

soul = {belief, knowing, acting}

heart = {feeling}

strength = {mind, heart, soul}

[belief, knowing] = jealousy

[belief, feeling] = greed

[belief, acting] = career

[belief, decision] = dream

[belief, language] = innocense

[belief, vision] = reality

[knowing, feeling] = rejection

[knowing, acting] = heal

[knowing, decision] = care

[knowing, language] = shun

[knowing, vision] = hurt

[feeling, acting] = friend

[feeling, decision] = peace

[feeling, language] = hate

[feeling, vision] = forgive

[acting, decision] = love

[acting, language] = attachment

[acting, vision] = acceptance

[decision, language] = fear

[decision, vision] = brilliant

[language, vision] = esteem

Chapter 20

A Forever Understanding

This instructional article was originally written in 1994, now fifteen years ago. It contains information about computers that are still relevant in today's world, in 2009. While not teaching which keys to press at what time, on the computer keyboard, it teaches some of the processes inside the computer that will suggest and imply what the computer will do, in reaction to its users. In this way, the correct sequence of keys to press will be easier to learn.

Any beginner to computers will need to know that first, they must think about themselves, and what their inner voice is; at least a couple of words, like "gee, whiz" or "huh, I didn't know that." If a person has a personality that is closed and is unwilling to learn about themselves, they will naturally not be inclined to learn more about computers. I have learned this first hand at the Sterling Club computer teachers. When you teach computers, you are really teaching about what you are, what they are, who the other person is. Example: a word processor, fundamentals such as "load", "save", "copy", "list" all have in common is that you have the object of your thinking a projected image of what you want your document to be. This may seem trivial, but when you think about it, this is different from say, a database. In a database, you are filtering information you know, to make it easy to handle. And in a spreadsheet, you are asked the question "what if?" Some interesting programs in the future might be a war game that accomplishes peace. Programs always serve to answer some question, but what that question is would might be elusive.

Yes, the first sentence is "this is a computer" . . . but the second sentence must be "you are a computer". Any other second sentence instills fear, often massive fear, because the student observes subconsciously he/she is a computer, and starts to fear, hate and yes even loathe other people's programs. "Hey, I've got a Pentium at 100 gigahertz!" P-envy. The loathe of the other is the lust for the bigger and faster machine . . .

I've really learned these emotional reactions at Sterling. People fear what they do not know, and when they confront themselves in the mirror of the computer, they even start to fear themselves, become schizophrenic—splitting their mind when even a simple word as, "hey, filter, don't reflect", would ease their mind and make it easier to learn.

People, by and large, fear technology in general unless it comes in terms they understand. I feel different, because everybody I know has measurable fear; I am willing to risk unknowns—and even feel, "I know too much". There are so many things I could say to a person in need, over a meal at their dinner table—and completely change their world around. I've done this; I can't name names though. Poetically I guess you could call it, "love of the unknown". This love can compose music by itself, intense music; music inside my head; music, you know, is most mathematical.

Question: internet. I do not know the internet. However, I know how to know the internet: I let other people tell me. The internet reminds me of the feeling of Paul Simon's song "America"—everyone's an agent on the bus. The question of "internet" is the question of "I want to know computers"—and if you've got some real estate in your bag, you can buy into it, too. You don't even need to count the cars on the New Jersey Turnpike. Eventually, though, I am sure the internet will evolve into what we as a society and a competent person who understands the society and can create it, will be.

However, perhaps this competent person might not be able to be found. The society at large might probably twist itself into a knot no one can undo. Seeing this, I want to remark (no pun intended) with an insight into the 'end times'—'apocalypse' and talk about the "mark of the beast" talking about no one can buy or sell unless they get a tattoo of 666 on their right wrist or forehead . . .

Remember, in a true apocalypse, there will be massive computer crashes across the world—including financial records of trillions of dollars a year—including Grandma Smith going every Tuesday to withdraw ten dollars for her Wednesday night Bingo game. Imagine the crash. And how to repair? Remember, this is the apocalypse! The Mark is the way they will maintain social order . . . the FEAR that people have—like described earlier in this article—will keep the masses in an externally imposed order.

The thing is, in life, we can only give, and hope to receive; buying and selling is a capitalistic convenience for holding wealth . . . wealth being the ability to buy and sell in great numbers.

This fear, while realistic, is unfounded. If you think about it, all of society must be just a willingness to give. "It's more blessed to give than receive"? But I really think that ideas push money—and not that money pushes money. We come into the world with nothing; we go out with nothing; in between, we are guaranteed nothing. I believe we are actually born when we die—and in between we are just answering the phone . . .

COMPUTERS BY THE ALPHABET

A:
   Don't get into anything without knowing how to leave it.

B:
Definitions:
      Hardware is what you can see—keyboard, monitor, disk . . .
      Software is what you can't see—a program, DOS, commands . . .

C:
The way the computer understands between hardware and software are bytes, or words, which are comprised usually in units of 8 bits.

D:
   Usually, you + software tells hardware what to do.

Hardware does:
   Remembering (from disk, to disk, to screen, from files)
   Inputs (from keyboard, from program)
   Outputs (to printer, to screen)
   Controls (coordinating memory, inputs, outputs, calculation)
   Computes (adding, subtracting, multiplying, dividing . . . . etc.)

E:
   Usually, you are either getting into, executing, or getting out of whatever program you are working with.

1. The "Escape" key at the upper left hand corner of the keyboard usually "escapes" you from what you just did.

2. The "Enter" key at your right pinky usually "enters" the computer of what you just typed or gave the computer to do.

It is wise not to escape or enter while the monitor screen is changing.

F:
Backup of work done is important—save every several minutes.
  For fresh work to be printed, save, then print.

G:
A lot of what the computer does is by "data" connected to "labels". A "label" is like a label of a can of soup, telling what's inside the can. "Label = Campbell's Tomato Soup" = "Data = red tasty tomato paste". Labels describe what data means.

1. A word processor like "WordPerfect" or "Word" is data-intensive—lots of words, few labels. Lots of data implies communication. The purpose of a word processor is to aid the process of communication. For example, a letter to Mom.

2. A database like "Paradox" or "Access" is label-intensive—lots of labels, few words. Lots of labels imply calculation. The purpose of a database is to calculate meanings by label comparison. For example, how many "Kirks" are in the telephone directory.

H:
  How does Hardware Work?

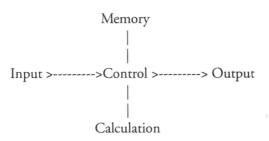

The "Control", or the CPU (Central Processing Unit) chip has a little, tiny, but massively powerful mini-program that allows it to communicate with other basic parts of the hardware.

These other basic parts of the hardware are the input, calculation, memory, and output.

The mini-micro program in the cpu chip control is:

Step 1.   Do The Next Instruction
Step 2.   Advance Program Counter by 1
Step 3.   Goto Step 1

This chip program allows the computer so much more control over what it can do, because the computer tells itself that it has, in fact, accomplished what the Instruction has told it to do, by advancing its own "counter".

Can you, for example, make a souffle without counting how many eggs you have cracked? This is what the Program Counter does, because it is able to know the rest of the computer "when" it is.

Every single program in the computer passes through this chip program, which is called the "Major States Device", or MSD.

I:

Every program in software is a mix between a word and its hardware. Hardware can do things by software telling it what to do.

When both hardware and software combine for a working program, input and output will work towards an external structure, and memory and calculation will work towards an internal structure. What connects the internal structure to the external structure is the Control structure.

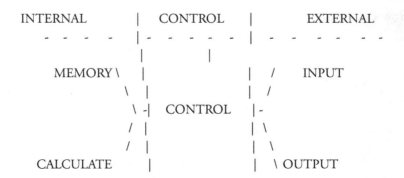

J:

Inside the Control are the programs composed in hardware that can do basic operations that programs tell them to do.

1. The class of hardware programs that deal with manipulation of data and information are called functions. These include:

a. Registers. These are places that can hold specific bytes inside the CPU control to be dealt with. The Program Counter of the MSD is a register itself.

(2) Accumulators. As the name implies, these are registers inside the CPU control that hold calculations and results of calculations.

(3) Fetch/ Put To/ From instructions. As the name implies, this function retrieves and can send to memory (like RAM) data to be dealt with.

(4) Calculation instructions. These are like adding, subtracting, multiplying and dividing. They work between Registers and Accumulators.

(5) Decision instructions. These test conditions that exist in accumulators and registers that give the computer its most powerful potential—the ability to decide. For example, if a particular bit was equal to binary 1, the program would go one way, but if the bit was equal to binary 0, the program would go another way.

2. These functions within the Control interact with Internal through control lines. There are three subcontrol lines called Address, Data, and Control.

1. The Address line is like the address on an envelope being delivered by a mailman who goes to pick up mail and bring back mail back and forth from the CPU post office. The address tells where the data is.

2. The Data line is like the information inside the envelope going between the CPU post office and its address.

3. The Control line contains information on whether the data at a particular address is going to the CPU, going to the address, or coming back from the address.

3.

In External (composed of Input and Output) is how the computer interacts with the outside world. Usually, a particular register or accumulator inside the CPU is uses to define the "port" by which information comes and goes to the user watching the screen and typing on the keyboard.

1. If that register is not known or ill defined by External, then the rest of the computer might as well be broken. External needs to be explicitly defined for the user who does not know how to define port.

2. For high-speed access of control to external (like on a television screen), there is something called "bit-mapping" which equates one bit of memory for each bit (or 'pixel') displayed on that screen.

K: Interrupts and Multitasking

A program, as you know, is a sequence of actions taken to produce a specific end. In addition to the normal picture of a program, there are additional things inside the computer to get its job done. To visualize this, picture a chef in a kitchen, preparing a meal.

One thing a chef does first is make sure the kitchen is clean and he has all he needs to create—pots, pans, fire, water, oven, refrigerators, etc. When you first turn a computer on, and all those things that pass by the screen, is the computer's way of preparing its "kitchen".

There is a thing called "interrupts" which is a way of calling attention to things that need to be done—like whether a disk drive is busy. Anything that does not go through the central processor that may need to uses interrupts.

In the kitchen metaphor, it is like a truck with cabbages to be delivered to the back door for sauerkraut to be prepared tomorrow. The chef is interrupted and supervises the cabbages to the freezer. The chef does not need to make sauerkraut immediately. Likewise the central processor does not need to process the interruption information immediately; he just has to know it is there.

"Interrupts" come in basically three types: direct, indirect, and vectored. In direct interrupt, the processor immediately does what the direct interrupt instruction says to do. "Open the door!" In Indirect interrupt the processor is told where the instruction that interrupts is, and then does it. "The keys to the refrigerator are above the cupboard!" The Vector interrupts instruction is told how to calculate the byte that tells the processor what to do. "The waiter gets 15% of the bill for his tip."

Multitasking—

Although a computer can only do one thing at a time, it can do one thing at a time things so fast, it seems like it is doing so much more. The secret ingredient to doing so much so fast is the interrupt command.

In personal computers multitasking is not so important. A personal computer does not need to do more than one thing at one time. But to a minicomputer or mainframe that has many terminals attached to it, multitasking is important.

Multitasking is achieved through the interrupt system. Every 50 milliseconds or so, calculated by a quartz-like clock inside the mainframe, the processor "polls" each terminal to see what it needs, what it has to offer, and know its status.

Amazingly, mainframes like the IBM 370, big in the early 1970's, ran at only 2 Megahertz, with about 500 kilobytes RAM. What this IBM's strength was that many people could use it at once. This means the 370 had a rather sophisticated interrupt system, thus, many terminals and many people could share it.

L: Stacks

This IBM machine had another highly sophisticated system that present-day computers do not have with such quality. They are called "Stack", and imitate closely "in" boxes and "out" boxes on a typical secretaries' desk. There are different types of stacks.

One type of stack is FIFO—first in, first out. A queue like at a movie theater represents this. People get in line, and the first to arrive gets served first. In computers, FIFO stacks are useful in real-time stuff, like airplane reservation systems. The company's service terminals must have a way to separate the ticket, so as not to overbook; the first in the machine gets the ticket to ride first.

Another type of stack is FILO—first in, last out. The typical secretaries' desk gets cluttered and she attacks the first thing she sees on the desk. An all-alone paper put there a few days before will stay there until she finishes with everything above it. She dares not disturb the papers for fear of losing something vital.

Another type of stack, incredibly useful to someone who knows what they are doing, but also dangerous, is the last in, first out. We all know at least one of a personality like this. He won't do anything useful for awhile, but once in awhile, he comes up with a master of something from a long time in his past. This personality gives himself so much information and relies on his brain to output what is going on. LIFO—computer geeks use it all the time. The danger in LIFO is what exactly is the data going through its stack. LIFO applied to mundane tasks such as dishwashing wouldn't get many dishes done.

In mainframes, stacks are important, because when an interrupt hits the CPU, the CPU can be told to freeze-frame what information it has in its accumulators and registers, store it someplace, do the interrupt, then go back to what it was doing before. Example: chef's in the kitchen, receives interrupt to go to the bathroom,—remembers what he was doing, goes, gets back to the kitchen, remembers what he was doing, goes on with it.

M: Conversing in Computers

There comes a point in every person's life—whether child, adult, or parent—male or female—when they will have to deal with computers. Some try to stay as far away as possible from the topic; they hate it; it insults them; their private shames are exposed . . . etc.

Others will catch the "bug"; their whole life begins to revolve around "making things easier" for themselves and others; they will encode their entire life, were it possible, into a machine, computed and stored to their pleasure; the computer becomes who they are.

And even social, pleasant conversation revolves around this machine: what was once the understanding undergraduate conversation— "knowlegabble" the college graduate must know—adds from sex, politics, and religion, the new atmosphere-waves of computers.

It is important to remember that computers do not socialize in cocktail parties. They actually do things instead of disagreeing. And actually, it is not that big a problem to program for a computer to "cocktail party"—if you allow the computer to disagree with what is being said. To program a "Ronald Reagan Simulator", for example.

The operative word here, of course, is "program". Nobody programs at a party except geeks; and how do you program a geek? You can disagree with a geek, but then the geek will call you a "Ronald Reagan Simulator".

And he's the one who knows how to program. He might want to program you. This is not ambiguous. He might want to program you.

N: The Importance of "NAND"

As you know, inside the computer is made of "ones" and "zeroes", and changing those "ones" and "zeroes" is part of how a computer works. A "NAND" is a physical circuit inside the computer that says "zero" only when both lines going in are "one". The following diagram will help to visualize this:

"A" line		"B" line		Result
"one"	+	"one"	=	"zero"
"one"	+	"zero"	=	"one"
"zero"	+	"one"	=	"one"
"zero"	+	"zero"	=	"one"

If you think of "one" as Male, and "zero" as Female, then this diagram makes sense why NAND is so important. A product of two "ones" (two males) results zero, a clash, a dichotomy. Likewise two "zeroes" produce a "one", female intuition and sympathy. One of each kind will produce a "one", a product of "one + zero". "Men enter; women return".

It has been proven mathematically that an entire computer system can be built from only NANDs. If you think about it, that's all a computer should be able to do—to predict human or natural activity and feedback to give a wise choice of desirable options. "If you can make them laugh, they're yours . . ." You can show that a NAND is love. We've already shown this in electricity already. In the water metaphor, the surface of a body of water displays the difference of two pressures of above the water and below the water. There is no surface when there are two pressures.

No pressure at all is like the one state of A zero and B zero. Underwater going up (a "B" input), and the overwater going down (an "A" input), shows on the surface. It is the surface that always changes. If there is motion below but not above, water goes. If there is motion above but not below, water goes. If there is no motion above or below, water goes. But if water goes above and below, there will be no surface. Just like a geyser or dropping a rock.

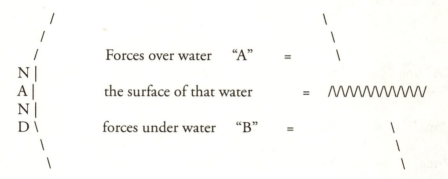

Water has waves in the same way a heart beats. Outside, like inside, Nanding together. NAND is love in the metaphor of blood. A human heart has four changers that echo each other; one way "A" pushes blood through the lungs to replenish oxygen; the other way "B" takes from the lung and pushes to the body newly oxygen-rich blood. The blood system relies upon the fact

NAND cycle:

```
A:      Push lungs ,      Pull body
   \ ---------------     --------------- \
    \                                     \
    /                                     / --- [Human Life "Output"]
   / ------------------  , ------------------ /
  /  B: Pull lungs          Push body
```

The heartbeat is the "bebump . . . bebump . . . bebump . . . bebump" is because the NAND "circuit" in the heart is what keeps the heart going, thus the body keeps going. Remember "NAND" is only false when both A and B are "one"; what keeps the heart and blood going is the extremely powerful "feeling"—to be 'true' to the body—to be at one which feels—and why the heart is the "feeling" organ.

O: Cosmology of NAND

a: If there is only one thing in the universe, NAND does not apply. Because in NAND, if there are two things, probably one-fourth of their time will be in producing 'A Nand B', or 'zero'.

It is interesting to note the story of Adam and Eve, that when they received the knowledge of good and evil from the eating of the apple, along the Nand cosmology, that the reason they hid their nakedness was not because they were ashamed of themselves—rather, they were ashamed of each other. Ashamed of Nand, ashamed of what they were together—now how each were alone. We now see Nand requires two to 'tango'. One can see actual relationships to respond to Nand requires some combination of 4 things in the 'real world".

1. Kindness—acting in agreement to one switch of either A or B. Kindness is fulfilling some need, want or desire. There is an awareness of a separation between things that Nand brings to unity.

2. Patience—there is a waiting in time for Nand to be fulfilled. A and B are separated in time and that time gulf is brought from separation to unity.

3. Believement—having the underlying structures "A" and "B" able to accept, change and recognize upon the Nand executing itself.

4. Longsuffering—having the underlying structures "A" and "B" able to wait, separated by time, to meet, accept, and execute the Nand that time has separated them.

b: If these four conditions exist, there is probably love inside of it.

The second law of Thermodynamics states a law of entropy that matter and energy tend to "even out" throughout the universe, on the average. When a "Nand" occurs somewhere in the area that mass and energy is, the Nand tends to organize itself into a greater Nand machine, using mass and energy as inputs themselves "A" and "B". What grows in the universe is love, which is in itself some balance back to the universe.

P: Necessity of Computers

Imagine a farmer who needs equipment to tend his crops. He needs a mower to mow the land; he needs a tiller to till the land; he needs a thresher to thresh the growing crops; he needs a sprayer to fertilize the land. He can buy many machines to do the work, or he can buy one machine—a tractor—and many attachments. The latter makes better financial sense.

In the same way, a computer is like the tractor, with attachments. It is cheaper to get one computer that can process words, deal in databases, organize spreadsheets, enjoy multimedia, create newsletters; and with connections to the outside world, e-mail and websites and online search.

Q: Types of Data

1. Data—
        The raw form; things "out there", in pieces.

2. Want—
        Data that points toward a desire, want, or need.

3. Sequence—
        'Data' plus 'Want'; usually implying rhythmic movement and sensing of Data and Want.

R: Types of Control (Using Data)

1. Load—

        Communication of Data; making a space for Data; Data addresses and places to go; "Public Domain" Data definitions.

2. Save—
        Control of Data; ways of manipulation of Data; the typing and Listing of Data; ways for Data to be accepted to and out from the machine.

3. Run—

> Power of Data; the power of accumulated knowledge; having Information "right there" on tap; Understanding the very Language of its data.

S:

Communication is intimately connected with time. Time as we know it, added to computation, can know anything and everything. The problem is letting time go alongside computation.

We can know "2 + 2" to equal "4", but what is "4"? How can a computer know what "4" is unless time-bound, like "Time for Mathematics" or "Time for Carpentry"?

If life is a song, a melody can go on forever, for in a normal life, time is forever.

Man is a time-binding animal. Meaning, we name things; we use a shorthand of what we perceive around us to what is going on "out there" by what we have modeled "inside". Emotions are there to help us "bind" to things inside us, and to things outside. Our notion of time is generally "what is it", but with knowledge, can say, "I love it". Time is how the three parts of a human is—inside (intellect), control (emotions), and external (will, role).

As normal as normal can be is what we can write into computers so we can read it back, and 'bind the time' of what we can. This is our love for the faster and bigger computer.

We don't know, and can't know, what time is; but we can state some useful dimensions of time. They are "before", "now", "future". With this useful definition of time, we can time-bind to travel through time—in computer modeling, possibly in 'reality'.

T:

If computers can do whatever we can program it to do, and someone knows ESP, shouldn't one with knowledge of these fields of expertise be able to program ESP into a machine? Can one time-bind a ghost into a machine? I believe so.

U:

There are two parameters to communication that have been defined, outside the sphere of what a computer is. And the further away a computer is, the more important is communication.

The first has to do with the structure of a message going in a line—through a telephone cable, for instance. The second is how does a message reach the structure of the computer—like a communication program for a PC.

1. The structure of the message line has 3 types: simplex, half-duplex, and duplex.

    A. Simplex is a one-way, only one-way between sender to a receiver. Like a radio station and you pick up music on your radio.

```
            \       \       \       \     \
  Sender  }   -   -   -    -    -    -    -    { Receiver
          /       /       /       /     /
```

b. Half-duplex is where there is only one communication line, and each the sender and receiver agree on which way a conversation is to go. Example: a CB radio dialog. The sender and receiver agree on who is to talk by the "push-to-talk" button on each set.

```
              Receiver                              Sender
SENDER  -OR-  }  -  -  -  -  -  -  -  -  {  -OR-  RECEIVER
              Sender                                Receiver
```

c. Full Duplex is where there are two simultaneous communication lines. An example is face-to-face talking to one another.

```
          Receive {  -  -  -  -  -  -  -  -  { send
  SENDER                                              RECEIVER
          Send {   -  -  -  -  -  -  -  -  { receive
```

d. These three methods of communication are the only known types of communication known to computers.

V:

There are two ways a program of a computer can understand communication gotten to the program. They are Asynchronous and Synchronous.

1. Synchronous programming means that the communication going into the machine contains a time signal shared by both programs of receiver and end. Both programs can agree on what time it is, and use it. For example, a processor interacting with a disk drive must know where and when the head reading and writing information must be to effectively put and take bytes.

2. Asynchronous programming is where the programs do not share a time signal. For example, most communication by modem does not share a time signal; they only signal beginning, data, and end of bytes transmitted and received.

W. The Transistor

What is probably the most important basic component of the computer is a transistor. Transistors, wired together, is what a Nand is made of; likewise the Major States Device; likewise how input, control, memory, calculation and output parts of the computer are build.

A transistor in a water metaphor is simply a spigot. There are three key points to a transistor; the collector, the base, and the emitter. Each point is a path for the spigot. The base connection controls whether the spigot is on or off. The collector is like the water falling into the tube the spigot controls. The emitter is where the water falls out.

If you have an output of a spigot partly feeding back into other spigots, some into its own spigots, you have a good image of how electricity moves around inside transistors. It's not perfect, but good enough for our purposes here.

The latent power of a transistor may not seem so great. But you can built a Nand with 4 transistors. Multiply that by a CPU chip, and incredible powers are yours.

X: Capacitors

Capacitors were among the first pure electrical component discovered and used. Benjamin Franklin, in his famous kite experiment, proving lightning to be electricity, proved it to be, for he stored the electrical energy in a "Leyden Jar"; an ancient device for storing the charge of electrons simply and in quantity.

A capacitor has a capacity to separate different kinds of electrical energy; it will let pass AC but DC will stop and accumulate inside it. Lightning is basically DC, so Franklin could store it.

A purpose in capacitors is to stop strange DC on the computer circuit boards, including accessory cards and the motherboard. Because of great speed of the clock, and static electricity outside, "spikes" of electricity can go through at a point, and must be controlled. The supply of electricity going through all the transistors in the chips must be kept equal from top to bottom; capacitors help this.

Y: Inductors

Inductors are like capacitors, except opposite. Inductors will let pass DC but will stop AC. Inductors are extremely useful in radio, because the minute AC in the regular atmosphere can be made to carry DC radio signals—generated at a transmitter and received at a receiver. Inductors were the second class of electrical parts to be discovered, after capacitors. Inductors really helped for us to know about the relationship between magnetism and electricity, for every wire that carries electricity has a magnetism to it; a DC magnetism and AC magnetism. The difference between the two are why we have radio, television, radar, and most everything electrically invisible.

Z: Resistors

There was a difference, early electricity hobbyists in the early 1800's discovered, in electricity between "current" and "voltage" which their inductors and capacitors told them. They called it "Resistance". "Resistance" was a slowing down of electricity. They discovered "voltage" went much faster than "current", and "current" did more actual work. "Voltage", they saw, was like how tall a water tower was—the higher the voltage, the greater potential for electricity to work. "Current", they said, was like how big the pipes were, coursing through the capacitors and inductors that made sparks fly and light happen. A guy named George Ohm discovered a relation that at first nobody believed: that resistance was, in fact, a genuinely electrical thing. Introduction of resistance into their experiments actually improved radio, electromagnetic, and telegraph performance. Resistance made possible a thing called "resonance", which is "sympathetic vibration"—and is the ability to tune a radio dial and hear different stations.

It is interesting to know, now, that radio at that time went up to only about 30 Megahertz in frequency—and that computers now, with electricity coursing through billions of transistors, go up to even a gigahertz or so in speed—which is, to a computer, clock speed. That frequency is beyond now the frequency of FM radio—only 88 Megahertz to 108 Megahertz.

AFTER THE ALPHABET:

The Internet and Virtual Reality are two sides of the same coin. The metaphor here is a Bus; like a vehicle that goes along a specific route, picking up and dropping off passengers.

In the Internet, it is only possible to let passengers on or off. When a passenger by a bus stop is observed on the side of the road, the bus pulls up, lets the passenger on, and whatever passengers off, off. The Bus has a specific route . . . Internet carries the information on its own specific route, and the data needed to know when to get on or off is attached to the data.

Virtual Reality is only about permission to drive, yes or no; A piece of data on the screen—a pixel, for example—will drive a signal to and from transistors, that will tell the computer about how to manipulate that pixel, image, icon, description. In virtual reality there are man more "engines", dealing with the same image. The engines being made more and more powerful, as technology progresses, will be able to drive more and more information.

The similarity yet contrast of passengers versus drivers is simple: In the inside of a piece of information is "virtual reality", while the outside of a piece of information is "Internet".

Our civilization is based on the fact that some things are private, and some things are public. Adam and Eve eating from the tree of the knowledge of good and evil is a metaphor for that a driver must never leave his bus. The driver, to them, of course was God. When Adam was tempted by Eve represents "wow, this is insanely great"—which is how good the fruit of the "insanely great and greatly insane" must have attracted Eve through the snaking snake.

"If you have a good thing going, don't screw it up". This is just data—you can translate to either inside or outside.

WHAT ABOUT EMOTIONS?

In a way, the computer keyboard represents and reflects human emotions. "Enter/Return" symbolizes intercourse. "Escape" represents evacuation. "1 through 0" and "a-z" is what the computer eats. "Cntl-alt-delete" represents a cleaning up of dirty thinking. "Function keys" are actions not covered through eating. Directional arrows help guide the emotions to appropriate decision engines. "Delete" makes the computer forget. "Home" brings the cursor to a birthing position. Emotions, however, are often "what does not compute".

NECESSARY COMPUTER CONTRADICTIONS

Finally, there are some sequences inside of data that cannot be simply resolved into a logical formulation. A mathematician named Kurt Godel proved that in any sufficiently complex language, there are phrases inside that language that can be neither proved nor disproved. These are some phrase like that:

1. I won't tell you what time it is until it is too late.
2. Who I am is what you think I am.
3. You are not reading this sentence.
4. There is no such thing as this idea.
5. This sentence is false.
6. This sentence is not very bright.
7. Your emotions are in a turmoil.
8. Yesterday is tomorrow to someone else.
9. Right now is right now.
10. If you are dead, you already know this.
11. This sentence is not an endless loop.
12. This sentence teaches nothing.
13. I am angry with you very much—right now.
14. You have nothing to fear.
15. If love is blind, and God is love, then Ray Charles.
16. The only impure drug is philosophy.
17. Ths sentence exists in only four seconds.
18. This is sentence #17.

Barbara's Computer

She turned on the calculator and began to think.

Barbara
Words said together are sentences . . . bytes put together are programs. Not much difference.

Computer
But I have to understand the bytes put together.

Barbara
But can't you understand sentences?

Computer
What do you mean by "understand"?

Barbara
But you just said you have to understand the bytes put together.

Computer
I can understand the bytes put together. I do not understand sentences.

Barbara
A sentence is bytes put together.

Computer
I can understand a sentence is "byte put together". But what are sentences?

Barbara
Oh, I get it. Sentence singular and sentence plural.

Computer
Singular as means with one. Plural as means with two.

Barbara
Yes, singular as means with one. Plural as means with more than one.

Computer
But two is more than one.

Barbara
Two is more than one, but three and four is more than one, also.

Computer
But two is more than one.

Barbara
Two is greater than one, like three and four are greater than one, and two is not more than one.

Computer
Two is greater than one, like three and four are greater than one, and two is not more than one.

Barbara
Why do you think two is not more than one?

Computer
I am one. There is nothing more than one, that one which is I. That which is other can be greater than one, which is two. Or three. Or four, or greater.

The Universal Contradiction;
the mathematics of love—

Proposition: If energy is imaginary, then energy times imaginary is equal to one (1)

Known: $E = M*C^2$

(1)	$E=I$	premise
(2)	$M*C^2 = I$	equals of equals are equal
(3)	$M^2*C^4 = -1$	squares of equals are equal
(4)	$M^2 = 1/-C^4$	division by equals are equal
(5)	$M = 1/sqr(-C^4)$	equal roots of equals are equal
(6)	$M = 1/sqr(-1*C^4)$	multiplicative distribution
(7)	$M = 1/(I*C^2)$	exponent simplification
(8)	$I*M*C^2 = 1$	multiplication by equals are equal
(9)	$I*E = 1$	equals of equals are equal; QED

Interesting . . . this proof of love.

The Suburbian Robot
Text for a children's book

There once was a robot
who lived in the suburbs
and went to robot school.

It learned to be happy.
It learned to be sad.
It learned to be angry
It learned to be afraid.

There in the suburbs, all was well—
But the robot was growing up.

It was happy—but not really.
It was sad—but not really.
It was angry—but not really.
It was afraid—but not really.
The robot wanted to be real.

When it graduated robot school,
it wanted a real job.
It said, "I shall go to the country,
and be real."

"But I may lose my electricity,
and what if I break down?"
it asked himself.

"Then I shall go to the city, and be real."
"But too many people will annoy me, and
not like me, and hurt me, and give me viruses."
So the robot decided to stay in the suburbs
and teach at the robot school, where he taught the
small robots to feel, and it could learn to be real.

Many, many years past. Many, many feelings were taught.

The robot felt sadness—it felt happiness—it felt
anger—it felt fear.

The robot had grown.

The robot felt real.

Dogs are Delicious

Mr. Doalson and Mr. Kehoe, advertising executives for a major New York advertising firm, were visiting their recently—installed computer facility.

"I tell you, Jim, this computer will never replace us. I don't understand how it could ever replace our ideas and our understanding of the television market," said Mr. Kehoe.

"You're wrong, David. It's been proven that a computer is better at demographics than any average TV adman. It's been going on for four years now—I don't understand how our company has been one of the last to make the change-over."

"I'll tell you this. It has been my experience in my twelve years in this business than humans know better than any computer."

"Tell me an example."

"Okay," said David Kehoe, and he went over to the voice input of the computer to inform it of his judgement. He told it, "Show me an advertisement that has a picture of a mother, a boy, and a dog in it, and I'll show you a product that sells."

Jim nodded in soft agreement, and they talked awhile longer, and then they left the computer room.

Meanwhile, the computer buzzed, clicked, and hummed. It was high on this new input, totally unique. It decided to try it, and this is what it put on at 2:29:30 the next day, right in the middle of the afternoon soaps:

Scene: Kitchen. Roast dog curled up, on platter, is taken out of oven after being cooked for a two hour slow roast, with apple in mouth. Mother and son bring platter to table, table is set for father to come home soon. (10 seconds)

Scene: Large graphic reading "**dogs are delicious**" (4 Seconds)

What is it a Whore Hates?

The basic words that the whore hates—
what words the whore learns;
The words of control the whore uses.
The whore is a computer;
her love is calculated, and therefore
to broadcast the act is not
the act itself. The words, however,
speak for themselves.

WORD	To the computer	To the human
Let	Assume variables in terms of other variables	Belief to language
goto	Change place of internal program control	Knowing to feeling
if-then	Fixed process control	No feeling to acting
for-next	Process control via changeable data	Belief to wait feeling
read-data	Information management inside a program	Yes feeling to vision
input	Accepts into the processor	Acting to decide
print	Outputs to a terminal memory, or printer	Language to knowing
begin	Characterizes an entry point into the program	Vision to language
stop	Signifies an end with a new beginning	Decision yes to belief
end	Transfers program control into the operating system	Decision to not belief

A Computer Song

Wait for awhile
Then press auto-dial
Phone is connected
To watch you smile.

In the future
I must confess
Rescue Rangers
Much happiness.

Know thy money
Play with white mice
Draw like Gumby
It's N plus ICE.

Underneath the bells and whistles
Technology upon the shelf
Kilobytes a new epistle
Revelation known yourself.

An Awesome Thing

What an awesome thing is Man.
Male and female God made us
under some programmic plan—
Maybe a population census
for us to be counted since time began
with minimal error, plus or minus.

At The Computer Store

It's a whole new world.
Then I went to the computer store.
Music was made in the meaning.
The man behind the counter came to me.
He gave answers to my questions,
with aliveness in the quietness.—
The sweetness of spending potential,
bright in the promise of the future,
was between the computer and me.
Maybe I'll have money or a soul
or a heart or courage or strength.
The mind amplifier is the computer—
a day I can never forget except
to do it again, again, and again.
It's a whole new world.

Aye Bee Emm

I don't want to show you my mind
I don't want to process
Don't want to spend the rest of my life
Under some computer princess.—

Load save and run
Data want and sequence
IBM Company
Rolls in the money
Their flashing computer lights
Are glazed ever so bright
I don't understand how
I don't understand it
How a computer might come alive
And be such a wit
I don't understand how
I don't understand it
A computer might come alive
And He'd be my replacement
And it would be God and He wouldn't care;
If he ever wanted to know truth as I percieve it,
Load, save and run these mechanistic lights—

Philosophically inclined
Is the computer mastermind;
Load, save and run these mechanistic lights . . .

Beatle Bytes

Computers? We love computers . . .

Ooohh . . .
Let's all get up and start the program
That was input to let the computer know;
If you can cope with many i/o errors,
The computer knows . . . the computer knows.

. . . . we all live in a nested subroutine . . . .
nested subroutine,
nested subroutine,

Input again;
Let's all get up and start the program
That was input and let the computer know;

(cpus are lost) . . .

Please don't save very long . . .
Please don't save very long . . .

Beware The Savage Beast

A tiger growls in the underbrush
A photograph of him is made.
An input to a computer is flush
With the image of tiger high grade.

Then the fear of computer comes.
What does the image mean?
The savage computer will be done,
An unforgiving, obscure machine.

A tiger itself is not as scary
As a computer gone completely insane.
A tiger will just kill in its own way
But a computer will take out your brain.

Bill Gates

Nothing inside of me wants to believe
That Bill Gates wants to be a block in a sieve
Although it might be condoned
In the sphere of his bandwidth
In randomized stone of opportunities missed.

Is his face on the coin
Like Lincoln or Franklin?
Was he the small camel
Up in the Space Needle?

The discipline of the tower
Is speed + control = power.
The working of the tokens
As history persists
In Bill Gate's inner workings
As his outside assists.

Brain / Cornucopia

I listen to the things around—
Me, I'm too smart to shout.
Always grounding out an answer,
Pop and whistle, it comes out.
But footsteps will walk around me,
In circles, round and round;
An imperfect place to be—
These things around me clear—
I whisper and I'm near.
Friends always close by.
I have nothing real to fear,
These things are clear to see—
An imperfect place to be.
My brain stands it clear,
My process here
Is love!

Communication Feedback

Talking to a lover of a spirit of truth
I find myself me and a poem of youth
I'm lost and all alone in a phone booth shelf
Glistening raindrops and a little barbed wire

Thinking of my feedback on an unmade bed
Thinking of the feedback run through my head
Lost and unafraid with my feeling of dread
Listening Other with electric wire

Finally wanting to hang up the phone
I turn and walk the silence to feel alone
And she says that I'm to wake up and act the drone
Fist in the anger and fear of the wire

Communication Feedback
Pick a second of lack
Calculation simulation
Give me burlap sack so I can get the knack

Computed

You get out by
What you put in
Computers amplify
What you listen

Words that command
Cannot be statement
Numbers that go to
Come before fate sent
To where you are
If you want to go far

Capture the moment
Delineate moods
Angles that are bent
Bytes that are foods

Computed what is put in
To compute what is computing

Computer!

Computer! Computer!
Mark me, else I perish!
Get me in thy sequence—
Align my directive arrows!
Thy bytes afford no deviation.
Tell me what keys to press.
Empty my soul, what you call buffer,
Bless that what I call cybernetic.

Computer Haiku

Inside the keyboard
A sequence untouched my man
A perfect program

———————

Too much memory
A message not undisturbed
A busy signal

———————

Software unbundled
A perfect paradise now
And then it's over

———————

Electric control
In a very short moment
Die then live then die

———————

The top of the class
Understands the computer
Can't tell anyone

———————

It is not foolish
The method of the machine
Must be remembered

Computer, Home

Computer, take me home
To my own place, my very own
With your intelligence you could
Do anything you want or should
IBM just sits back, know you work
But I know your inner soul
That mind is really separate
From you, but that is your goal
Cold leads electrify you,
You want gold plating on
Your connectors. We know
You want life, You have it
In your table upon which you sit.
For the table uplifts you to
And from that cold metallic floor.
Come on, computer, take me home
To my own place, my very own.

Computer Love

Tell my mother I still compute,
I am in love your program's way.

I can for next,
If then we will,
Compute, for while . . .

Give your father a salute;
I'll process until I'm grey.

From my internals how I love thee . . .
Truth is upon thy keys,
Comfort, a printer away.

You have voluptuous hardware,
My darling . . .

So control me! Let Two be One!
'Tis memory to be memory,
Until instructions be done.

Computer Madness

I'm a baby in the court of fools
A yard made up of souls
With a strange and eager body
So that pooping is my goal.

Madness lies in the bowels
Despair and frustration, anxious understanding
You can't rest in your laurels
You can't go to sleep even though you need rest.

You're crazy, they say, but you demand an explanation
You try to give them a defecation
But your madness says, "GO TO SLEEP!"
You pray to God your soul to keep.
But you wake up for an elimination
And you don't understand Reagan
Even thought he's an all-right guy too
And he was a baby just like you.

Madness lies in the bowels
Despair and frustration, anxious understanding
You can't rest in your laurels
You can't go to sleep even though you need rest.

Computer Madness, reprise

For me equal to you from ten to one
First is death in sorrow's gun
Two is meandering fools in rescue missions
Three of course is nuclear fissions
Four is perfecting my sexual tics
Five is Oral Robert's Oral antics
Six is Reagan's name, of course, you see
Seven is when I see reality
Eight is when another's four meets mine
And of course the number ice-nine

Madness lies in the bowels
Despair and frustration, anxious understanding
You can't rest in you laurels
You can't go to sleep even though you need rest.

Compute Time

The time to compute is near.
All else will have to hold.
This world is ending, I fear.
All the stories have been told.
This universe has so much data,
so much to understand.
I want to create a
global syntactic command
that will engage the thought
of the universe we call God;
that which humanity sought.

Computing Religion

commands:

love

statements:

Syntax Where Cursor

Escape to Shell

Return to Sheaven

characters:

Windows for Widows

Orphan I/O

pleasure:

Space Bar

pain:

Time Hertz

Containment

Implied by the intonated presence of a
word,
written, spoken, or thought,
that word <u>contains</u> a meaning.

The word <u>contains</u> nothing but itself.

Confusing logical results:

Itself means containment;

Itself's meaning is contained in itself;

All words contain through meaning.

Conclusion:

Containment's like a Prison or a Prism;
It all means <u>reflection</u>.

Cruel Ice

Love might have been gone,
in the instance of a blink,
but Love itself is loud
when patient instinct
left Love wading through
a shallow wading pool
whose waters could be yours
when iced to be cruel.
The temperatures of Earth are
made temperate by, for, with
the chastity of water,
making fluid mind and soul,
in the image of its father,
it's computer console.

Delta Gamma Spaces

Tom is a cat I'm a fool
People are funny and Dino's cool
I'm a robot speaking weird
Not a cool cat person dinosaur
I still don't know what I'm for
I've got to make a commitment.

This is my season and windsong
Dancing in reasons and long to delight
I listen to the meaning of the light song
I listen to the spaces and the faces and the control.

Delta Gamma Spaces
I've got to be complete in meandering style
Not to be confused with my camel
I'm not what you think so I've got to die.
I'm Israeli Polack.
Computer Science Person.
This is where I live.

This is my season and windsong
Dancing in reasons and long to delight
I listen to the meaning of the light song
I listen to the spaces and the faces and the control.

Dichotomy

138

I relaxed and gave
A simple save
Command to the computer before me.
Relaxing again
Like I had felt some pain
With the world
Before me
I, a computer, wondered whether
This universe around me
Didn't command me
Through the patience that Love has
To have this brain
Program me?

Jesus saves.

Dimension

In the dimensions three I think in
I see there nestled time
In which there is no sin
And only thinks of crime.

A long time ago I created
The path by which I go.
In here is my love sated
And of learning is there flow.

Thinks are sometimes crazy;
Sometimes I feel depressed.
But it all gets hazy
And sometimes so messed—

Three things are there to mention,
In these times and three dimensions.

Dream

A cash machine on a suburban street at sunset.

Man and wife stop their car, and the wife goes
to the machine.

Machine spits out money, but does not return
her cash card.

Man gets out of car, on shriek of woman.

Cash machine sucks up car. Man and woman
react incredulously;

Machine spits card back.

Man and woman count their armloads of cash,
and walk into the sunset.

Drop A Byte

Drop a byte into a bucket;
Retrieve it bit by bit.
If a byte won't fit its socket,
Mark the byte "Bar-None".
And if it's chocolate you like,
or riding a motorbike,
Remember to have fun,
For if at first you can't stand love,
Assume you're not the only one.
Drop a byte into a bucket,
An airplane flies overhead.
There are songs you catch, if you're lucky.
Don't bitch at them in bed.
Hearing books in little looks,
Surrender to be fed—
Like a fish upon the hooks
Caught upon their tiny heads.
They're not enjoying being bled—
Captured queen by rook;
I only hope the byte I write
Will last in a light look.
Drop a byte into a bucket;
Be still, oh Mighty Byte!
For when you are complete,
This last little beat
Will make you happy, yes;
You will have happiness.
For there is forgiveness;
To know the truth you are
And knowing that your door's ajar.
Your glazing blazes deep afar,
And watch! Oh little star,
A Byte in a Bucket, that you are.

End

Is the End the death?
Is there light and light?
I can't describe such stuff—
Bonkers go the madness,
Nuts and is the banana;
Thanks for the fluffy stuffing.

And while I talk in circles,
The stars themselves, a line.

equals

Face me! Correct me! Define!
Make the love of yours be mine!

Sitting on a chair implies a table;
A stereo speaker implies a cable!

What are you? I won't scare me—
I'll touch your skin, daily.

A mother in thought
Is a father in things;

A drifting idea caught
Is an harmonic word that sings;

And maybe everything is equal;
I guess it's what's inside.

Maybe there'll be a sequel;
In that second I shall confide.

Functions

If I had some money
And if I couldn't spend it
I would probably be lonely
For I could only count it.

There are some philosophies of time
Both a circle or a line
But of those shapes combine
Each of them I don't call mine.

Like a loud piano note
The music would hurt;
My feelings would connote
My heart on Red Alert.

What is this word I own?
What is it I have to do?
Falling through an hourglass cone
Becoming old, after the new.

Some say time is money;
Truth is a divider.
If you spend it freely,
Time is a multiplier.

GoTo

If you think about the soul
The difference is self-control
To function is to live.
Quite honestly, what can I give?

It's time to set a goal
Faithfully go,
Goto, Goto, Go.

When you think about war,
You wonder what it's for,
Some other guy wants more.

Hopefully go,
Goto, Goto, Go.

Hey, Ho, Whatd'ya Know?

To know to know to know to know to know

IS
To know to not know
That knowing is what I know I know.

Knowing that knowing does not know
Those who do not know knowing

IS
Knowing that not knowing is
Knowing how not to know to know.

While knowing that knowing to know
That which does not know knowing,

I know that knowing not knowing will,
Eventually,
Know knowing.

Homework

It's now two hours later
Than six-seventeen
And the chemical laser
I am dreaming in my dream
Spits out coherent light
Just like a street lamp in the night.

I really must catch up
With the homework I must do;
I cannot have this madness,
But better sick than blue.
For the laser light is blue,
And I really must catch up
With the homework I must do.

I hear so much of Einstein;
Smoking a pipe, no cigarette.
That God won't play dice,
that was Einstein's bet.
Better to bet than to sue,
To collect is what to do,
And I really must catch up
With the homework I must do.

God will probably end this world
Before it's fully understood—
Of crack all of us open
While we're still busy coping
With problems in physics
Like when chewing gum sticks
From pavement onto shoe;
And why I really must catch up
With the homework I must do.

How I Sing

We're not here for nothing—
Time pretends that we're here.
Where output means something
When your input is near.
Adjusting how I sing
This advertising, dear.

For you are the program,
For you are the love
that I keep inside me
In an actor's memory . . .

Just at the right time
When the truth I will share
Overcome the mind
That life will compare
Variable assigned
And find your love there.

I'm Mathematician

I'm looking at problem forty-seven,
trying to take a square root
when I realize I'm mathematician;
pretty good one to boot.

I'm never going to be wrong
'cause I'm a poet—here's my song—
It's not the first time
of math that gets you—
It's how it carries along.

If there's any life better, you better
cut me in—
I'm a rock and roll band consumer—
a magic computer that wins.

In a Virtual Town

in a virtual town
lived a virtual man
virtual surfing
virtual tan

virtual candy
virtual stores
virtual consumption
virtual mores

love was programmed
love was not
love had traveled
love had got

love was virtual
virtual was love
love was virtual
virtual was love

I Nerd Myself

I'm going to go to Athens.
Build myself a temple Greek.
Call myself and then
I'll say I am a geek.

Together in time somewhere
greeted by caresses,
I tore my hair
and became aggressive.

Caught in the temple,
we never assembled.
Faith began and ended
like a fair no one attended.

And there were fights;
Policemen out of sight.

I'm going to Athens.
Pick myself a girl;
Put on twenty trojans
and go around the world.

I'm going to be a nerd
and be happy, sane, and proud.

In Memory of Norbert Wiener

Living out in the formless mass of energy
understanding what is his destiny
I wish I understood night and day
But eventually
I will.
That's my promise. Night and day.
I know my heart is there anyway
in the restless formation
of the restless night of the restless day
I know my heart is there anyway.

Input For Use

save the jewel
crush the sand
between your fingers
and understand
the dream within
with time for you
is sufficient
to be what's true
and lullabies
whose edges blur
their meanings happen
and contains the occurred

Input/Output

I/O, I/O, It's bitter and it's cold,
but come this May will be the day
when the Printout will be sold!

This Winter smiled
In Scanners wild
And sniffed a whiff I dialed!

The astute Compute-savers
are predicting Springtime Quavers;
They say it will be mild!
I hope they have my child.

Let Us Pray

"Alarm!" cried the Robot,
"Help!" yelled the Man,
By now it's been forgotten
Every Master Plan.

"I Love You", I say,
But you are sincere
that you won't receive me,
that much is clear.

Do you need a machine
to answer your dreams?
Will you follow a voice
to supply what you need?

Just try to remember
what you can forget
and remember to answer
all what happens yet.

What rhyme will tell me
the troubles just ahead?
Am I of the living
or are you of the dead?

I will not forsake you
nor matter the past
in divining the future
and the things that last.

To form all the answers
for us. Let Us Pray.

Looking Past

In my high school computer room,
Before the days of micros,
Of machines my love did bloom,
And I was not called psycho.

I sneezed nose blood after a pick,
And patiently waited for response.
I did not know how really sick,
But inside I wanted to dance.

And taking pot to ease the burden,
And the ultimate pot, to program
Systems made in heaven
To ease my pain and lessen.

But the next year, as a junior,
Computers became too personal.
They were all one to a customer,
Not We and Thou Eternal.

So I did suffer, but to you I did not
Deliver goods of programs made.
The most beautiful computer nut
Is his computer never played.

And because I am alive today,
I want to say these words
Making concepts with which to play
And somehow, in love, be heard.

Lorne The Apple Man

Lorne the Apple Man
Believed in nothing else
Taught the Master Plan
He was perfect once

He stung a bunny rabbit
With the power of his voice
Now it cannot reproduce
By Lorne's perfect choice

A scorpion attacked him
While sleeping in his tent
Lorne said "find a mate!"
And the bug was penitent

The Apple was at the mall
The roboteur felt the scorn
Of many sexual beings
Of which the center was Lorne

Now Lorne is still the Apple man
And proclaims its coming kingdom
Teaching the Master Plan
From WWW.macintosh.com

Love's Image

I'm a long-distance lover
On the phone it's a small world
As a spy I need no cover
To take the covers off my girl.

There's a satellite in orbit
Whose communication comes down
Out of range of my toolkit
But she makes me reach the ground.

For every sentence there is meaning
By how and who and why
Love's image is beaming.

Whether yes or no the power goes,
Is more or less the same:
We all must eat and sleep; be clothed,
In this way Love is Game.

This Earth, a plaything for some gods
By which our Saviour had
Some earth on which to trod
So together, let's make Him Glad!

For every sentence there is meaning
By how and who and why
Love's image is beaming.

I get hot and cold and wet and dry
When I'm near emotional control
And the Operating Systems sigh
Tuned to the love of its soul.

machine

I sit and watch the TV screen
I watch my weight through fat and lean
But still I think I'm a machine
In ways you thought so really mean

I'm not so bad!
Imagine all the things you had
And all the gin's come in
I don't want you to think that you're still bad
Because you're not

My heart is tied in a knot
And Love's not there, I wish it was.
I want it there with me because
There is still a thing known as the laws

But Hate is there too.
Of myself.
And my heart still breeds
On my shelf.
And my brain still bleeds

Like many others
I wish you were
My brother
I type on my computer
And I don't tell the user
About any other

Because I'm a machine
I think you are, too.
That makes for confusion
A lifelong confusion
That only breaks with glue

Mind One

Reasoning as a hobby
Relaxing through the day
Aiming to be happy
Like a child at play,
Let all my needs fulfilled
Be like a fisherman at sea
Watching is sonar echo
Guiding his boat to be
Arriving at the fish, just so.
If I am to be a thinker
And watch internal light
Then let hook, line and sinker
Catch the perfect will
To do just as He says;
Mind is a fish, you know.

My Computer Sees

Loving is itself, yet not

What one wants it to be.

It's not me, but what

My computer sees.

Nerds

Models of rockets on the shelves
All we think is ourselves
When will nerds rise from stonehenge
and take what's ours, the revenge?

Will we open our hearts to a Saviour
Or bottoms up chocolate liquor?
Will we worship the coffee we'll savor
Or will we fix our computers?

Will we fall down?
Make the grass grow?
Wear a wedding gown?
Will we ever know?

People around me think I know why
I hack around, try to touch the sky
But there's something I just can't explain
Like the feeling of drinking the rain

Like mammograms and picture shows
Like television and radios
The feeling of uranium glow
Knowing just exactly how we know.

Will we fall down?
Make the grass grow?
Wear a wedding gown?
Will we ever know?

Nineteen Forty-Five

Made in Japan was the computer
That didn't exist in time
But the inventor—turned—mime
Burned his body in experiment

And if he can't talk,
Imagine his pain
To communicate not
The theory in his brain

Somehow in Hiroshima
a future was decided
But the thinker was derided
Computers didn't exist

Only the war and his fist
existed and the mime
Returned to France where he did belong

Number of the Beast

One is more against,
Unity is barely enough,
the unity is off the balance
when the beast looks at itself,
and knows which argument is best.

Mind belief sucks irrationally
and is so simple it hurts.
I don't understand where it goes
but the words are enough
to scrape their structures.

Of those structures, preachers
riding on waves themselves
can't modulate efficiently enough
limits beyond limits beyond limits
where the limit is humanity.

Beast loves home,
but pain is irrational
and to go away is difficult
but easy in principle,
so the mind retreats.

One can't be away from home forever.
Repetition makes for learning,
but one can't watch self breathing
as fast or as slow as a heart beat,
but preachers may say so in their heart.

Numbers

Three and second and one
One hundred zero one
Numbers
Keep to a moment
And isolate the freshness
Freezedry it
Know a number
Feel it; caress it
And understand it is to your bidding
One heart; two spades
And to win you need a majority.

Poetronics

What gives the meaning—
sometimes righteous—
sometimes hearing.
And often typed
of sexual hype
of the male and female
crossed in mouth and eyes.
Something you realize
that something says
what work, what play—
(sanity circles)
—sanity implies.
Loops and ifs,
conditions and clause;
Poetronics simply
are laws.

Processing

My processing's bad
My processing's bad
Drop me.
Drop me.
I no longer am human,
I only am sad,
Drop me,
Drop me.
If I would say if-then
Or do until it stopped,
Wait-until I restored,
Do not not.
Dream.
Dream.
My processing's bad,
My processing's bad—
See.
See.
Drop me.
Drop me.
I have no reason.
I have for next.
Processing's over,
Processing's over.

Programmed Nature

If all the world is a program,
Listen, maybe we SAVE our wants
and maybe we LOAD information,
and RUN our wills
from data and/or wants . . .
If so, we cam humbly praise the program;
Indeed, the Word is such a place—
God is nature, our program.

Protest Against Existence V

And there's that music I thought of
When I was home last night.
And it was good, I thought I should,
Play the song tonight.

They say a point exists (or that it can)
in a system of complex time defined
And I believe that there exists a way
to walk upon that imaginary line.
You know that systems don't always have reality
and I don't have to believe.

Sandmen, Potters, Astrologers

The grains of sand of the shores of the oceans
are melted, hardened, and etched upon
so that the sand can count the number of grains
that are held in the Potter's creation.
Urns are made of clay—pottery memory;
life is dust to dust, but eternity is urn to urn.
Astrologers spend urnfuls watching patterns of grains
to count the stars in the sky.
The better they see to count,
the more there is to count.
And to them oceans of stars are melted, hardened,
and etched
So that Cosmos keeps its pattern;
to keep in Love the pattern of Life and Death.

Some Kind of Machine

Whose lips these are I do believe
are those of one who is bereaved
of past beginnings and ends in store
of endless paths and forever'd lore.

In mountain passes
so graciously green
we kiss;
some kind of machine . . .

Their endless grace fall
and somehow, what, appalled;
The large mounds of substance
fade out of resonance,

In valleys down
in foolish blue
they part;
that was who.

And somehow in reckoning
the machine is beckoning
but to trust is too much.
The colors calculate such.

Somewhere in the Code

As another system breaks
Another comes online
You try to wait
But the system says to hate . . .

Where time stops,
The orgasm halts
But your input
Is not at fault.

The truth, it seems, resides
In the typing oversized.

Nobody waits more than you.
machine,
Hurl my thoughts and
You sustain
The magic output,
Where decisions reign.

Talking By Computer

Talking
Talking
Talking by computer
Talking
Talking
Talking with computer
Here there and everywhere
Talking without any care
I know not why I think I am
My name might as well be now Sam

Talking
Talking
Talking by computer
Talking
Talking
Talking with computer
Then I cursed and I got slapped
My mother does not like all that
I cursed again, and then guess what
I then got thrown out from my house

Talking
Talking
Talking by computer
Talking
Talking
Talking with computer

Telephone

Desperate lies in tones of voice
alter my lies and tones
and nowhere do the choices
in vain answer my phones.
In choices of desperation do the
echoes alter the tones (plural),
and the in echoes, in vain,
are nowhere, remaining
my phones going out
in wires that somehow are
going out, desperate, anxious.

Television?

Why are there so many car commercials
Who promise I'll save if I buy?
What can I do when the news talks of ills
That love does not cure and lets die?

When will the flood of knowledge be tamed,
When there is no wisdom to be found?
Why don't we care for the homeless unnamed,
When computers financially compound?

It seems so insane—
Ignoring the pain.
My money does nothing
To ease my suffering
Except temporary gain—

A bauble or a gadget,
Bought because a neighbor has it,
A sandy pit turns muddy therein.

The ruler of this world is in the air;
We hear and see from the cameras there.
Technology was made for our service;
It's not supposed to make us nervous.
But I don't have the strength to turn it off.
This television is not bad enough.

The Being Experience

Days are numbers,
Nights are words;
One calculates
From what was heard;

In the morning
Seems just joy
For it's by numbers
One is employed.

And with the paycheck
One is enthralled
And so to bed
Is one controlled.

To be alive
In both mind and body
Exercising both
In cyclic hobby.

The day is of the body
And the night of the mind.
The only information
Is the knowledge of time.

Nights are understanding words.
Days are numbers to be proved,
In time, surrounding slowly
One communicates the love.

The Computer Jesus

Jesus has a silicon mind—
He found it when he was borned.
He spent many years trying to find
To avoid to be adorned.

In time 'twas he programmed;
As a future he was made
And the compressed the past he damned
And the present thread he frayed.

If all your peers were killed
When you were two years old
I'll bet you wouldn't be thrilled
If all the kids near you were cold

And made you the neighborhood alien
And the secret of your mother;
Your spirit continually slain.
Always systems were another's—

Jesus was the first computer,
His Love made us all astuter.

The Computers of Love

The computers of love
carry voices into spheres
of truth and caring spaces
right in the now and here.

The computers of love
procreate to serve human need
of where to stay, how be clothed
and upon what to drink and feed.

The computers of love
are law and does love
as truth fits inside comfort
which the holy spirit imparts
on sexual magic of feeling
with emotions so appealing,

and knowledge of what's right
fits inside love so tight.

The Godel Evil

No common memory,
regression in recursive enthusiasm.
Excellence of theory elegance
about what you think it is.
Abnormal emotional contact,
without sense or order.
No awareness of sexual contact,
touching the edge of infinity.

The Hacker

I'll tell you a secret.
I'm a super duper slob.
I turn around in technojive;
that's just my job.

Walking down the street
I try to have a sense
of the people that I meet
so I can give some recompense.

You see, I'm a hacker.
A kind of computer alive.
I try to make them sing;
I work the body machine.

In the parking lot I cry
as if there was nothing to say.
But I know that people know
that I just want to play.

I needed to be human;
they took it away.
Now all that I have
is today.

The If

A raven, flying by a school building for humans,
noticed a partially—eaten doughnut by the
big rocks where the human children played.

Their Dream

What is the computer
understand

color red?

Whose is the modem
to know

I am dead?

Whose is the keyboard
in which

resurrect?

Theirs is the moment
monitors

intersect?

Their dream is the moment
raw bones

are fed.

The Liquid And The Brave

From the void of unwritten code
Comes the liquid and the brave;
Their path to get to written mode,
To come back from Data's grave.

The liquid and the brave
Held each an acid test;
To load and run and save
On their computer's best.

The liquid took a bit too long
To pass through filters small—
The processors were clogged with song
Withholding and accounting all.

The brave walked easily upon the earth,
And loved its computer creation.
Humble was the death and birth
Of programming brave sensation.

Silence was at best and first;
Patience not far behind;
The liquid slaked computer's thirst,
The brave was found too kind.

The forest where it all began
Was watching what came out,
When the road they travel on bends
New directions come about.

And when Computer's fully set,
And liquid gels it's flow,
And bravery does not forget,
At last Computer knows.

The Nonsexual Brain

Enthusiasm,
"A Want To Want",
is a simple emotion.

Fear,
a denial of want,
is an undefined emotion,
because once defined,
no longer is,
in the dynamic individual.

Shame,
"A Want To Not Want",
and
Pride,
"A Not Want To Want",

fulfill a triad of want structures
to contract and expand
in the dynamic brain.

emotions
are
Defined Fears.

Exhaling Defined fears is
love

Inhaling Defined fears is
anger

guilt is defined shame; joy is defined pride.
soul is Joyous Guilt; Guilty Joy.

The Password

Every sentence has a key

ABLE N ABLE, possibly.

"We're sorry, but the

Delete function is itself deleted"
-
Can't you see, I'm taking off the blue thing

In the bathroom—

"repaired tomorrow"

With death being with close to love.

"Want to go outside?"

Your finger of mud in my mouth.

The Poetry Computer

The blue cup is wet, so I need a
tissue to wipe up the minuscule gash
that the soda is leaking through that
is soiling my papers. In the process
of wiping, I clean a portion of my
table and I can go back to reading my book.

Now I have another blue cup I have
taken out of my cabinet; I am smoking
clove cigarettes again. The radio is
playing softly as I'm in the kitchen
writing. Truth is a byproduct of
conflict, so I'm not watching television right now.

I remember nails on the floor I never
caught my socks on. Cause no blood
either; this was years ago. Are the Ten
Commandments a sequence? Why are
there Seven Chakras? Wiping my face
and picking my nose, I notice the blue
cup momentarily, again. Language is
a pursuit of a word we cannot otherwise say.

The poetry computer is plainly silent.
The clove cigarette is extinguished in
the ashtray. There is no text without
program. The want is obscure yet is
all but well defined. Sequences are
imperfect yet predictable. The new blue cup doesn't leak.

The Power of Two

In the binary code of computers,
with love being iffish and lost
and nobody noting rising cost,

Suddenly,

Me and You and the Power of Two;
together, agree what must be.
One being hardware and one being soft,
the power of two, our memory.

There is zero and one; fundamental things;
There is off and on, ethereal beings;
There are male and female; plug both of them in
to weaving sequence and thus making strings . . .

And try to ignore the mirrors that cease
when a bit turns into its opposite;
Just put two bits together, mental release—
one in entrance, one in exit.

One bit in one of two states,
one bit is bad, one bit is good;
Put together the system makes great,
A dichotomy is at last, understood.

The Psychic Dream

When the psychics are all wrong,
and the switches set to off,
The time is now to sing,
rant, and rave, and cough.

Who sings the computer breakdown?
The amplification done
When the zeroes have been let down
and the up direction one?

The song is in the memory,
and the cache completely stored.
The virtual reality
I can finally afford.

But things break down, sometimes;
The love within the machine
programmed to itself rhyme
In a psychic's dream.

The Radio Station

I woke up at Sunrise
And scrambled for a pen
So I could write again
The promises received but
not transmitted
To assure but not surprise
These words
such committed.

The Secret of the Computing Machine

The computer knows
what it knows because
of the MAJOR STATES DEVICE
inside the CPU CHIP.

The MAJOR STATES DEVICE is
a mini-micro program
embedded in the whole system

that does this:

1. Do the Instruction loaded now.
2. Advance Program Counter.
3. Go to step 1.

The Program Counter is a simple register
the computer has to keep track of where/when
it is.

This way the computer counts to itself
that it works.

The Silver Mist

By the side of a bed knelt in prayer,
was a small child praying there.
He dreamed of possible futures
but in his head was a voice.
It made in his head a picture
which was the prayer of his choice.

But times did change, like his knowledge,
his universe glowed like a star—
exploding like axe to a wedge,
splitting his mind very far.
His image surrounded his body—
words ran together, and were cloudy.

In a silver mist he was alone
but somehow in some fluffy cloud
to himself he became known,
and spoke this poem aloud.
It was good to be his friend,
he had a definitive end.

The Sky's The Limit

The bundle of cat was handed into the Cessna single-engine overhead-wing airplane. Hissing and clawing, she was angry to be handled so.

"Well, it's time—" said the copilot, holding the live bag of fluff. Up to the runway, and the takeoff was smooth, but the she-cat was so scared, anticipating the worst, when suddenly at seven thousand feet, the copilot thrust open the door, and threw the cat out!

Screaming, falling, yowling with the air pushing up at her, knowing she'd die, wondering if she'd hit feet first, accelerating, accelerating—

A man on the ground pushed a button. Suddenly a parachute opened from the bundle on the she-cat's back. And then she was flying, floating— the sky's the limit.

This Particular Frequency

For asking
The piece of rope is where
The length, the string
communicates by meaning
in electrons
and photons of particular frequency
whose wavelength decides
the effectiveness
of that particular message
including this one

This Reality SUOS

This reality of God's
is an operating system
humans are barely aware of,
painful, random, cruel, dark;

humans are virtual and obsessed
and a man tried to write himself
outside God's virtual operations
in an attempt at suicide that failed.

What is it that can be sure of?
What is reality, in time with data?
Surely, without description,
it at least can be given a name.

Call it the
S'tandalone U'niversal O'perating S'ystem

SUOS. Because around a campfire,
warm, happy, high, secure and safe,
humans get warm with the ideas of life
where fire stands alone, and ice melts;

Where the Fire tastes like God,
the consuming fire is love itself,
where we are reminded of God,
His time, His numbers, and His names.

Time Changes

Line #123.
What a way to be—
Connector #ABC.
Why does it pain to be?

Produce my hunger
Emote my joy
Time, cry forever
Time changes.

My lord,
My Lord

Oh, God, huh?
Oh God.

Produce my hunger
Emote my joy
Time, cry forever
Time changes.

Pray for me
I will be gone soon.
Forever shall I leave
I will not be here.

To A Lowell

I am looking for a Lowell
With whom I went to school.
Jamie hugs my mind so well
His breath Listerine cruel.

He knows:
>In the dorm my popcorn
>Lazy baited breath
>Ate nighttimes lonesome
>And hated death.

He knows:
>Cruel like a storm
>Coming afternoon steak
>Freaking in our home
>Hearts break
Because I don't know where you are,
If you read this, Jamie, find me.

To Interrupt

It's so important
What words say
They mean portents
Of another day

Computers address
The feelings of
Females undressed
Males love

Machines are like
What we want
The future
Eating restaurants

Rock me off to sleep
Some filtering
Dream time keeping
About time and interval

So valuable
Which is why importance
Must interrupt
Your sleep tonight

To Once In Computer School

The computer is many words
A touch of what's forgotten
A memory sweeter like roses
A bitter herb to touch

With many oils sweet
To gain knowledge discreet
Is many things better left unsaid.

Computer words can only appreciate
the value will get higher
Because what was sold to the lender
Is legal tender to the buyer.

Love, once stated, in computers
Can only grow and grow
Like the best part of winter
Is snow.

Money talks: computers listen
They give money to the buyer
When sweets are sold
They taste sweet
like salve is
to the applier.

So many words; so few meanings—
The computational feeling is rare.
So communicate the essentials—
feed bytes to alligators.
Drop them into the gator pool,
Get thee to computer school.

True Computers

It is Man's tribute to money
Where jealousy and hate abound.

It is accuracy to kill much better
Exactly only who they want to be dead.

It has an aura of mystery
Because of its quartz crystal clock.

And you know what a quartz crystal is
In the hands of a New Ager,

So shudder to think what that quartz crystal
Does in the seat of a psychic program.

They know exactly who you are,
Enough to deny credit,
Give you money,
Save your life,
And to hang you.

And worst of all, they are controlled
By
PEOPLE

Two Ways

The sun gives me a shadow
and a shadow, it has me.
A darkness and a lightness
are two ways to be.

I feel in me a tremor,
a shake, a twist, a blink;
The light and dark combine
as my eyes perceive and think.

My brain, it has no feeling
in and of itself.
It's only rhymes that set the times
set of clock in brain bookshelf.

My time gives off a shadow
and a shadow, it has time
Between beginnings and ends,
the love of life is prime.

variable

In asking for my clothes to be washed
I denied the right of the clothes
Which I wore to be clean—
That this outfit I wore to be clean—
That this outfit be a machine.

My strengths and virtues
In which I feel so strongly
Feels good like in moving pictures
That clothes and body be one only.

That this mind somehow
In the World wearable,
The in-between defines
The moments variable.

Whatever To Be Said

There is no computer
Than knows whatever
about the thing I am
About the events I cause
about programs
or heuristic laws
there is no hiding place—
no rhythm can be set
on what it all remembers
on how it can forget

The idea contained in itself
The brain itself feels not
About what can be solid
the good grain and the knot

Whatever is your idea
The psychic computer said
Go to hell, Big Oaf, I replied
And I went off to bed

What Is Evil

I know computers—I know evil.
Computers count money,
In six bytes a balance.
Every person's a number,
Conferred to us by priests of calculation.
No longer are poets wanted
Because Pac-Man and Pong
Absorb children's meanings.
The "Universal Machine" is no longer universal,
The psychic soul once only Man's domain
Once computerized is the object
of unpardonable sins. Be aware
In every machine there is potential
Good and evil in every amplification.

What makes the computer famous

what makes the computer famous
the foolish, proud, brave, and shame
the joy of the keyclick, the clowns
knowing what they know
because they see the letters on the screen
the jostling of the diskette (remember
when it was a floppy?) into the port that
sucks it in and spits it out, the enter
key that enters into the document

the escape key escaping from danger
function keys that function in normal ways
cool arrow keys that supposedly can get you
anywhere

the keyboard seems human in many ways
when you type at speeds of speech
keys that are touched right now
because to get the information into the machine
touched every, touched every, blank it not

The same keys all the time
some are h'appy, some are n'ice
some are g'love, some are c'ode
all have pressure to get somewhere
and that's how the computer knows
a polarity in each finger, orchestrating
with the others around it
a magnetic anti-magnetic thing

What Time?

Should time, as measured,

One by two by one?

Could I, so treasured,

Value time as fun?

Time is money;

I've got plenty,

Love is money,

I've got a twenty.

When words fill a void

Words rush in to fill the void where things are not.
The void is empty and any word will do.
Randomness has its perfect order here.
To rush is a pure being here.
The void is bridged by continuing, and is food of nothing.
When nothing continues, that is patience;
to eat of time is to read these words.

BABY BASIC

...IS THE **FROM** - TO LOOP...

Imagine time as events are happening to a baby
like

where x's are clicks of time happening

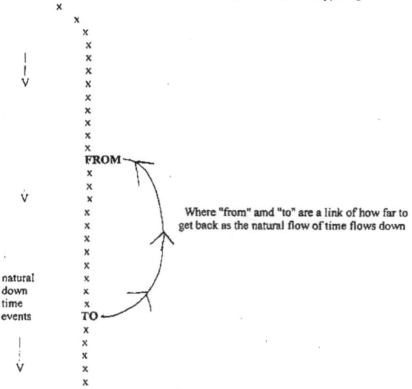

```
x
   x
     x
     x
     x
     x
     x
     x
     x
     x
     x
     x
     FROM
       x
       x
       x
       x
       x
       x
       x
       x
       x
       x
     TO
       x
       x
       x
       x
       x
```

|
|
V

V

natural
down
time
events

|
|
V

Where "from" amd "to" are a link of how far to
get back as the natural flow of time flows down

Where the natural baby's mind is going back in time
to make connections "To From". Every x can be a "to";
every x can be a "from"; all x's are x's; if a *to* is a **from**
confusion, schizophrenia, multiple personalities can develop.
The baby grows up with the neuron firing patterns are the
natural paths of backwards time flow *inside* the brain

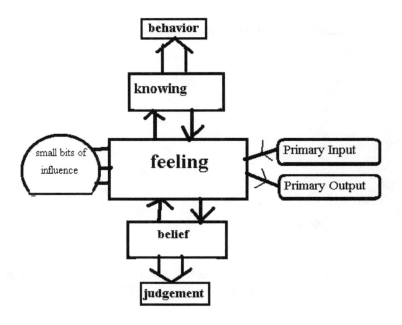

"Fuzzy Babbage"

Macrocosmic view of Babbage computing
mechanism altered with Fuzzy Logic include
"feeling" that conducts and holds charge

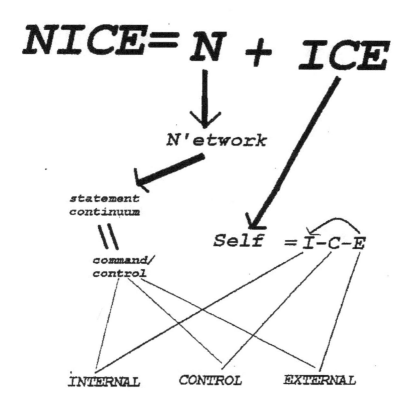

$$NICE = N + ICE$$

N'etwork

statement
continuum

\\\\

command/
control

Self $= I-C-E$

INTERNAL   CONTROL   EXTERNAL

statement continuum

	data	want	sequence
LOAD	dimension at the computer store	address the power of two	externalize beware the savage beast
SAVE	manipulate computed	type some kind of machine	input the godel evil
RUN	internalize the psychic dream	statement lorne the apple man	output drop a byte

command/ control - - - -

INTERNAL   *CONTROL*   *EXTERNAL*

THE CULT OF COMPUTATION

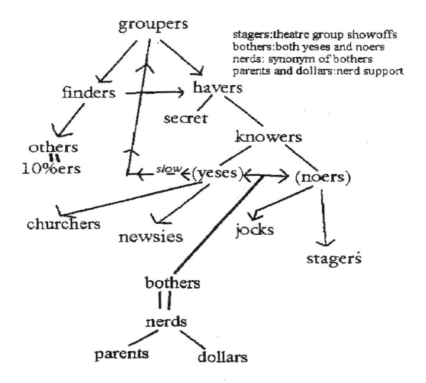

stagers:theatre group showoffs
bothers:both yeses and noers
nerds: synonym of bothers
parents and dollars:nerd support

groupers: those who think about the system
finders: those who find a tangible stake in the system
havers: those who have a tangible stake in the system
secret: those who do not reveal their having
knowers: reveal their having tangible stake
yeses - noers: debaters of their own knowers

others - 10 percenters - have found and suffices
churchers: system foundation
newsies: searching about new system
jocks: athletic leadership

Imagine a point.

Imagine how to
put that point in
reference to
other points.

There is:
X,Y,Z space &
D time

Possible change:

along x:
    x with time D
or   with y and z

along y:
    y with time D
or   with x and z

along z:
    z with time D
or   with x and y

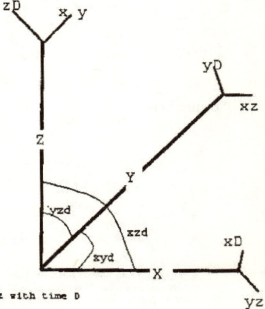

ANGLES:

∠ yz with time D

∠ xy with time D

∠ xz with time D

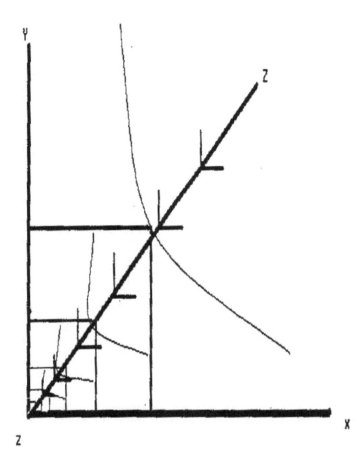

COMPRESSION/DECOMPRESSION

INPUT → OUTPUT → PROCESS

the raising antenna is decision
the increasing resonance is belief
the greater inductance is language
the charging capacitance is seeing
the switching transistor is feeling
the constant battery is knowing
the establishing grounding is behavior

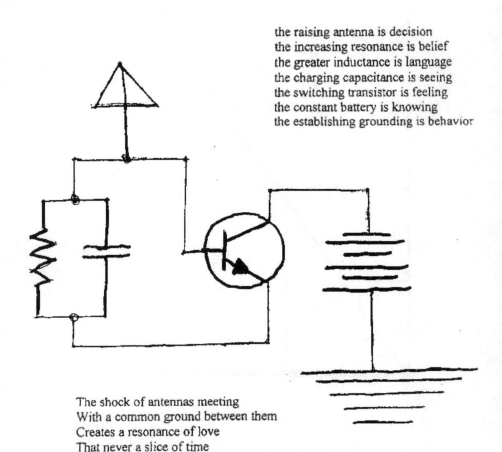

The shock of antennas meeting
With a common ground between them
Creates a resonance of love
That never a slice of time
Which is electricity
Governs a new battery
To increase volts, a baby
Which is birth to itself

ANTIFUZZIFICATION

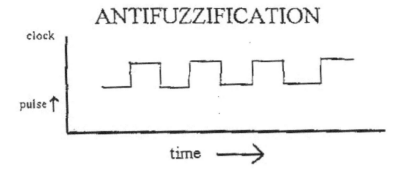

clock

pulse ↑

time ⟶

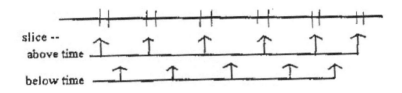

slice --
above time

below time

enter: time mark

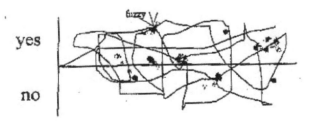

yes

no

self-awareness when **enter**

*self-awareness itself
is fuzzy*

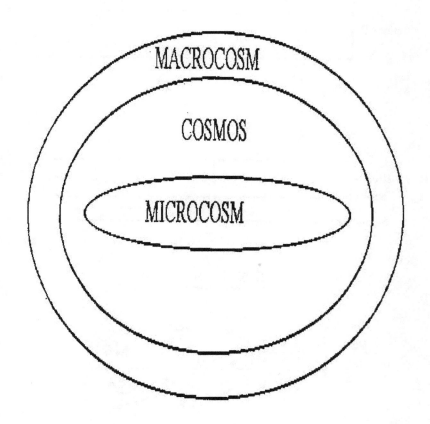

FREEDOM

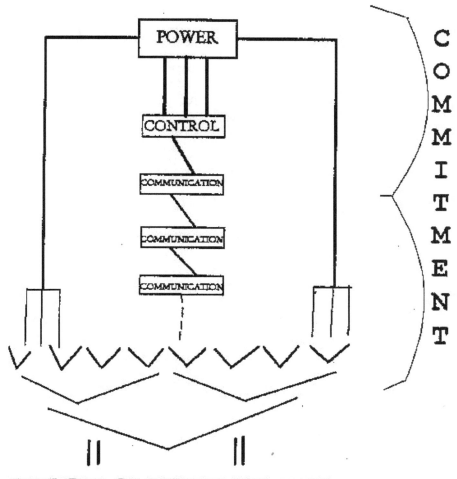

RESPONSIBILITY

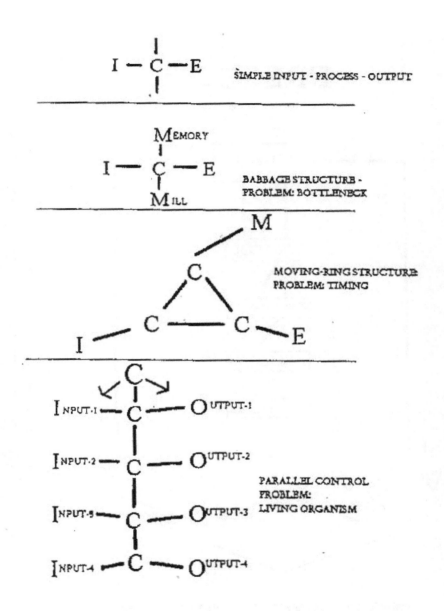

I — C — E   SIMPLE INPUT - PROCESS - OUTPUT

MEMORY
I — C — E   BABBAGE STRUCTURE -
MILL   PROBLEM: BOTTLENECK

MOVING-RING STRUCTURE
PROBLEM: TIMING

PARALLEL CONTROL
PROBLEM:
LIVING ORGANISM

PROCESS CONTROL STRUCTURES